Sketches

Alvar Aalto

Edited by Göran Schildt
Translated from the Swedish by Stuart Wrede

The MIT Press
Cambridge, Massachusetts, and London, England

Originally published in Finnish as *Luonnoksia* by
Kustannusosakeyhtiö Otava, Helsinki, and in Swedish as *Skisser*
by Söderstrom & C:o Förlags Ab.

This book was set in V-I-P Optima by DEKR Corporation. It was
printed on Warren's L.O.E. Dull and bound by Halliday
Lithograph Corporation in the United States of America.

Library of Congress Cataloging in Publication Data

Aalto, Alvar, 1898–1976.
    Sketches.

    Translation of Skisser.
    1. Architecture—Collected works.   2. Architecture,
Modern—20th century—Collected works.   I. Schildt,
Göran, 1917–   II. Title.
NA2500.A2213   720   78–6155
ISBN 0–262–01053–4

Contents

Foreword

A book about architecture by Alvar Aalto—for everyone who knows the Finnish master such a book must appear a paradox. His untheoretical bent, his focus on real construction instead of abstract speculation, was of course from the beginning the personal trait that separated him from the other pioneers of the new architecture. While Le Corbusier, Gropius, and Mies van der Rohe expended the main part of their energy on polemics, education, and clarifying the practical reasons for breaking with old stylistic traditions, Aalto represented the quiet creator of projects that spoke for themselves. To a certain extent this had its cause in the age difference: he took over developed principles that the rationalists had had to reach by themselves, and he could, unburdened by hidebound tradition, continue on from the positions already conquered. That is why he was such a remarkably unpolemical innovator; he is in his character totally free of those constraints that tempt protestors constantly to convince themselves and others of the despicability of the past.

When Alvar Aalto passed away on May 11, 1976, after a short heart illness, he was by no means finished with life. The work in his office in Helsinki, where twenty or so younger architects were employed, continued at full pace. He had recently inaugurated a large theater building in Rovaniemi; the working drawings for a church in Lahtis (now under construction) were in process; and he himself was preparing to travel to Tel Aviv, where he had been invited to design a concert hall of approximately the same size as the Finlandia hall in Helsinki. In Italy a church he had designed was under construction in Riola near Bologna; from Germany delegates came to discuss the final details for the opera building in Essen; and in Finland the town council of Jyväskyla had approved the funds for a new stage of the extensive city hall complex. These were only some of the projects in progress and plans under discussion.

For Alvar Aalto this extensive activity was nothing unusual; he almost always had this many projects on his drafting board. There are, of course, architects who have built more buildings than Alvar Aalto, but few have produced such a wide range of public buildings, including everything from city halls, churches, universities, museums, theaters, concert halls, libraries, and administration buildings to hospitals, assembly halls, exhibition pavilions, department stores, and restaurants, in addition to the whole scale of housing and industrial projects. Already in 1927 Aalto was simultaneously involved with such demanding projects as the building of the civil militia's hall in Jyväskyla, the church at Muurame, the theater and labor union building in Turku, and the design of two projects that would shortly make him known abroad, the Turun Sanomat building in Turku and the library in Viipuri.

All these buildings were daring innovations that broke with the established taste and met resistance from conservative circles. That Aalto, despite this, was allowed to realize them was due to a great extent to the open architectural competition system in Finland, whose juries consisted of highly qualified professionals. It was also due to Aalto's unique ability to gain people's sympathy and convince the doubting. But the most basic favorable condition was that he began his professional career at approximately the same time as Finland became independent. There was a large demand for buildings in the young republic; the desire to build up the country literally found its expression in both public and private architecture.

If we compare Aalto to some of the other major pioneers of modern architecture we can say that historical circumstance gave him a good turn, while, with equal arbitrariness, it cut off Gropius's and Mies van der Rohe's promising careers in Germany and relegated Le Corbusier to working in a conservative France that had more than its share of monumental architecture. Aalto was, in other words, born at the right moment in the right country.

In the 1940s when he was a professor at Massachusetts Institute of Technology in Cambridge, Massachusetts, he could have pursued a career in the United States, as his older friend and colleague Eliel Saarinen had done a few decades earlier. It would appear superficially that he turned down an attractive temptation and chose the path of sac-

rifice when he in 1948 returned to Finland. Now, afterwards, it is easy to see that in the United States he would never have oeen given such many-sided projects, so well suited to his social goals, as those that awaited him in Finland. This does not mean that his contribution would have been less useful if he had chosen to stay in the U.S.A. Aalto could have become a factor in the process of self-criticism and renewal that is the admirable and hope-inspiring side of American cultural life. There was much in the United States that appealed to him, primarily, perhaps, the optimism about the future and the pragmatic grasp of reality that he associated with the frontier tradition. He was childishly amused by the wild customs in the old gold-mining settlements, by the cowboys' straightforwardness, and the improvised social life of an unsubdued nature, which the books and films recount. All this appealed to the anarchistic side of him, which was a holdover all his life from his boyhood days. On the other hand, what he took exception to in the American life style was technocratic hubris and dollar worship. This doesn't mean that he was a Rousseau who dreamed of a retreat from the aberrations of civilization to nature untouched (by technology). The architecture that denies industrialism and attempts to reach back to the past's idyllic aspects was foreign to him. There is no doubt that he regarded technology and industrialism as positive phenomena, as it is only with their aid that man can build a humane and just society. On the other hand, he saw the dangers that threaten if technology is allowed to serve short-term profit motives, the ruthless exploitation of nature and the evil desire for power. These phenomena are of course old companions of mankind, but it is only since technology increased their effect a thousandfold that they have become truly dangerous. The task of humanizing technology was to Aalto the fateful question of our age, one that is also expressed in architecture. What above all he wanted his buildings to exemplify is how modern technology and a humanistic conception of life can be brought together in a convincing synthesis. It is an architecture where technology is systematically relegated to a subordinate, serving function, instead of being granted the naive homage that characterizes so much of modern architecture.

The other aspect of prevalent tendencies in the United States on which Aalto took a critical stand was his suspicion of or aversion to money as the regulator of development. It is clear that here there were deep rooted influences from his childhood at work. His father, the land survey engineer J. H. Aalto, and his grandfather on his mother's side, forester Hugo Hamilkar Hackstedt, were both civil servants who did not have to think about making good business deals, but rather pursued their jobs as impartially, faithfully, and professionally as they could. Despite the fact that Alvar Aalto worked as an independent architect he succeeded all his life in maintaining this elevated attitude toward economic questions. He was never concerned about whether or not a project was economically advantageous for him, and he refused to work for clients who primarily had short-term economic goals in mind. He viewed himself, in short, as a servant of society of essentially the same nature as the traditional disinterested priests, doctors, judges, county attorneys, foresters, surveyors, etc., who in the old Scandinavia were public servants. In his private life this meant that he allowed himself a standard of living that approximated what a higher civil servant might enjoy, but never amassed a fortune and throughout his life maintained complete integrity.

As for his attitude to political questions, his stand required that, in the manner of the civil servants of the past, he regard himself as being above political parties and class differences. He never voted in elections and in the 1920s had already built both a clubhouse for the politically rightist "civil militia" and a people's hall for workers, just as in the 1950s he built the Communist House of Culture in Helsinki at the same time as the large church in Seinäjoki. This did not mean that he was indifferent to social questions. He was regarded in the 1930s as a radical architect on account of his strong focus on the social concerns in building minimal dwellings for the masses and in worker-oriented industrial planning. He was a member of the international architectural group CIAM, whose social reform program influenced his work to a great extent. Socialistic architects such as Gropius in Germany, Hans Schmidt in the Soviet Union, and Markelius in Sweden were among his close friends. When he talked of architecture he held up the classless society as the goal without a second thought. But he maintained a doubting or critical attitude toward the self-righteous, mass-oriented social experiments that have been carried out by force in different parts of the world.

Alvar Aalto is famous and his work has been written about, but no thorough study on the man and his work has been published. His biography is unknown, except for the public data; the catalog of his projects is incomplete; and his buildings have been only sparsely analyzed. Brilliant viewpoints have been put forward by, among others, Robert Venturi in the U.S.A., George Baird in Canada, A. Ikonnikov in the U.S.S.R., and Nils Erik Wikberg and Pekka Suhonen in Finland, but they only touch upon individual features in Aalto. An important publication is *Alvar Aalto: Complete Works*, in three languages, based on Aalto's own project descriptions and illustration selection, edited by Karl Flieg and published by Artemis publishers in Zurich. The two volumes already published present Aalto's more important projects from 1927 to 1970, and a third, which deals with Aalto's more recent work, is being put together. The Italian architect Leonardo Mosso's *L'Opera di Alvar Aalto*, which was originally published as a catalogue to the Aalto exhibit of 1967 in the Palazzo Strozzi in Florence, is still, with its adequate building descriptions and its extensive illustrations, the most complete handbook on Aalto's total career. A series of important works on Aalto can now after his death be counted on, among others, a study by the American David Pierson on Alvar Aalto and the modern style.

It is not difficult to explain why so few major studies have been published on Aalto's work. It is due to a large extent to his hesitation to give out archival material and his disinterest in all research concerning his earlier buildings. He deflected questions about the past by saying that he was interested only in the projects he was currently working on. This attitude should not be interpreted as modesty or as a lack of proper sense of self. Aalto regarded himself as without question his own era's most important architect, since no one else better filled the demands he placed upon architecture. On the other hand, he categorically rejected nineteenth-century artist worship. He was against what he called the "cult of personality" and therefore wished that what was written about him should concern the objective qualities of his buildings, not him personally.

This attitude was reflected in his designs in such a way that he never wished to make manifest a personal artistic expression, to leave behind him monuments to himself, but rather to concentrate totally on creating the best building the client's program and the exterior circumstances allowed. This explains why his buildings, despite a very personal vocabulary, do not become too subjective, but rather stand out as adequate and in principle generally applicable solutions to our era's building problems.

Alvar Aalto considered theorizing about art or culture to be easy and in no way binding, while creation was the difficult and important activity. Therefore he devoted all his energies to creating concrete examples of what he regarded as a correct way of building, while he never bothered to write a book about architecture. This didn't mean, of course, that he would on principle refuse to express himself about general artistic questions or individual projects. On the contrary, as a hyperintelligent observer, reader of literature, and a lively conversationalist he lived with words and ideas as constant companions and intellectual tools. This side of him even lured him in his youth into sporadic appearances as an art critic in the daily papers. Shortly his architectural activities took over, putting an end to his writing. His presentations of his projects to clients, competition committees, and journalists were always full of ideas and often elevated themselves into pure literature. The word-artist came to the fore even more clearly in the speeches and informal talks that conventions, social occasions and openings of exhibitions lured or

forced him into giving. Aalto was recognized as an excellent speaker who, unhampered by written notes, freely improvised during direct contact with his audience. These talks were sometimes taped, but showed themselves in written form impoverished of a great deal of their content, as so much lay in the delivery itself, in the tone of voice, the hesitations, expressions, in short, the experience of going on an exploratory trip in a complex reality with the speaker. Most of Aalto's speeches are as such unpublishable. In certain cases, demands from the arrangers of the symposium, requests from the editors of architectural reviews, or other circumstances got him to tolerably rework his speeches into enjoyable written form. Sometimes also an interviewer succeeded in drawing a consistent declaration out of him or in fixing his answer on given questions.

It is a selection among this almost accidental literary material that is presented here for readers, texts by an author in spite of himself, the definition of thoughts that never strove for a clear definition except in one area, that of architectural creation. And yet this editor doesn't feel that he is betraying Aalto by making them available in book form. A critic has every reason to present a body of material that not only aids in the understanding of the architect's work, but also illustrates general changes of focus in the architectural debate from the functionalist breakthrough of the 1930s and the fight against the new modernistic formalism to the questions of our time concerning the destruction of the environment and psychological alienation. Alvar Aalto has in all these questions been a radical pioneer and a dependable guide, not least because of his sharp eye for social realities.

There is another reason for publishing Aalto's texts. His method of reasoning—never categorical or authoritarian, constantly open to objections and amplification, colored by a fine irony and genuine humor, yet, despite the apparent searching, so sure of its goal and so full of creative vitality—is actually exemplary both from a literary and a human viewpoint. The tone is that of conversation, of dialogue, not that of magisterial dictum. It is a text that in many ways has the same qualities as Aalto's pencil sketches. It has therefore appeared to be appropriate to publish a generous sampling both of his nature sketches and his architectural sketches within the same covers.

These sketches, like his oil paintings and his sculptures, performed a truly central function in his creative process. It is not a question of some lesser branch of his artistic talent or some compensation for the limitations architectural design involves. The landscape sketches and annotations on the buildings of the past are rather a kind of spiritual exercise, a putting into practice of Aalto's basic method: to filter clearly perceived separate entities through the unconscious so that a viable synthesis arises. Just as the singer constantly practices his scales, the athlete keeps himself in training, and the ability to use language is maintained through constant practice, Aalto trains his eye for the complicated interaction of visual forms. The goal is not to create artistic sketches or interesting paintings but to train the sensibilities. The sketches and the paintings, to which he devoted a considerable part of his time, were only means of reaching that control over architectural forms that was his main goal.

The majority of Aalto's sketches of nature were done during travels, which is quite natural, as travel in a particular way stimulates one's impressionability and allows time for purely aesthetic interests. The sketches were done in sketchbooks of various formats, which for decades lay forgotten in Aalto's drawers, of no interest to him as their function was only to come into existence. Many such sketchbooks have surely been lost or have not yet been rediscovered.

Of the sketches published here the oldest are from his first trip to Italy in 1924, and a good many of the others from a trip to Greece in 1953. They show how his modernism received inspiration from the old Mediterranean cultural tradition. The sketch from Pallastunturi in Finnish Lapland is from the 1930s; those from Cape Cod date from 1946. Morocco and Spain he visited in 1951, Egypt in 1954. The fantastic, almost Leonardoesque sketch of the volcano Heklas's eruption came into being in 1947 during a trip between Finland and the United States in one of the slow airplanes of that period, which gave Aalto time to capture the mighty view out of his cabin window.

As far as the architectural sketches are concerned, they are chosen almost randomly among the enormously rich material available, with the goal only of giving an understanding of the variety and the aesthetic qualities that these working sketches contain, created as they were without the slightest aesthetic aims. About this material one can say generally that the sketches from the years before the war are closer to conventional architectural drawings than the sketches from the later years. The free, ruthlessly private character of the latter is due partly to the fact that they were made for very trusty collaborators who subsequently clothed them in what was for the client a more accessible mode.

The essays included consist of only a selection among the Aalto texts known to the editor. I have primarily focused on texts with a humanistic connection, while more technically oriented texts have been left out and variations on subjects already treated have been avoided as much as possible. The year the texts were written and the place they were first published or verbally delivered is provided after each text. Alvar Aalto reviewed and approved the publication.

Motifs from Times Past

Admiration for, and a deeper knowledge of, our old, indigenous architecture and our former values would appear to be of a relatively late date in this country [Finland], but so deeply rooted among us "professionals" that we are now actually finding in them a basis for our own work. Yes, I suppose one can say without reserve that it is precisely the authority of the past that is the main criterion for our work today. Besides, it is a goal of the public information program [in Finland], whose purpose is to better the public taste (which must also be seen as one of the architect's essential duties), to prepare a favorable climate for modern architecture by attracting the general public's attention to our older architectural culture and to underline its ideals and aesthetic values. Research on our older architecture and the publication of its results is in full progress, we may note with satisfaction.

In this connection I would like to dwell on some characteristics of certain examples of our older architecture by emphasizing some particulars of form.

When we visit a medieval church, look at an old manor house, or contemplate a hundred-year-old vernacular building, we find that there is something that reaches out to us, a mood. It may be caused partly by handcrafted surfaces, by the building materials' artistic purity, by the simple lines that harmonize with the landscape; partly it is created by the materials' one-hundred-year-old patina and fine worn surface.

I am led to believe that most people, but especially artists, principally grasp the emotional content in a work of art. This is especially manifest in the case of old architecture. We encounter there a mood so intense and downright intoxicating that in most cases we don't pay a great deal of attention to individual parts and details, if we notice them at all.

And yet there is something that deserves to be placed on a par with this mood, and that is the architectural motif, the modest stylistic signature that one sometimes comes across in both primitive and more developed examples of Finnish architecture. I remember well with what pleasure my architecture school class "attacked" the only limestone portal in the old monastery church in Naantali, a portal conceptually quite daring for the Finland of its time. Not just living stone, but living *forms*. *Style*. Here we met architecture. It was a stylistic creation as he had experienced it, this Nordic builder who created the portal. It was not just a case of traditional building skills permeated by the master mason's pleasure in his work; it was an artistic creation made by an architect. The mind always reacts in the same manner when we encounter a stylistic motif. Let me take something from a later period, for instance, the small hall in Olkkalas manor house with its almost Tuscan column decorations, or the almost comically humble double staircase at Wadstena castle, which Professor Romdahl enthusiastically called the Renaissance's first messenger in the North.

So rare are these stylistic motifs, especially in the older architecture of our country, that for that reason alone they are valuable pearls; but at the same time they signify a great deal more. They crystallize distance, the fact that our country lies so far from the centers of culture. But their artistic value is not reduced by the fact that one often hears them labeled with the meaningless words "provincial art." All phenomena of this kind in our older art are in character as Nordic, sometimes as Finnish, as we could wish, and yet they occasionally show us the *international artist* within these, our ancestors.

Perhaps it would seem unnatural to treat separately these stylistic motifs, details in the totality of our older architecture; on closer inspection, it seems impossible. But one can, with a faint, hardly legible theoretical line, define on the one hand that in our historic architecture which is inherited, which has developed gradually from generation to generation, and which is essentially based on any one era's technical achievements, having its roots in climatic conditions, standards of comfort, and indigenous aesthetic traditions. On the other hand one can distinguish something that we can perhaps call architectural luxuries, in other words, everything that has been added as a result of exterior influences, of impulses from afar, sometimes brought directly from abroad, whether in the form of a detail or merely a feature in an architectural whole.

My purpose has been only to underline the stimulating effect of these currents from abroad on our art. These "luxury motifs" have gradually exercised their influence and given fresh impulses to architecture that perhaps was created by a provincial master with skills passed down through generations. The confidence of the architects of the time and the very modest conditions prevailing in our country are attested to by the fact that these motifs, even in their earliest versions, appear to be in total harmony with their surroundings.

When our modern architecture quite recently was under the influence of the Swedish Vasa renaissance it was above all following the example of this "master masons' craft" in our older architecture. It was a period of admiration for handicrafts, and when town planning, that most developed child of our time, put an end to this period, a final benefit, our esteem for materials, remained. Now that the indigenous Empire style has again been raised to an aesthetic norm we have a richer choice of architectural motifs. We have begun to worship our architects of the past since we abandoned the skilled master mason, surely a direct result of the fact that we feel the great limitation of our national art.

This does not mean that we should reject all that we have learned from the indigenous characteristics of Nordic architecture. Nor is it an indication of weakness or of a small nation's constant emulation of larger ones. Rather it implies a true understanding of our country's past and can be seen as a definite strength, because now no local European style or personal theory (Morris or van de Velde) can pull us into its vortex. Now we are setting our own course. And when we see how in times past one succeeded in being international, free of prejudices and at the same time true to oneself, we can with full awareness receive currents from ancient Italy, from Spain, and from modern America. Our ancestors will continue to be our masters.

"Menneitten Aikojen motiivit," *Arkkitehti*, 1922

Housing Construction in Existing Cities

Die Städtebau has entertained its readers with a series of articles on the architectural ideal city as it has appeared in different so-called master projects. Buonarotti, Vauban, and a number of others appear in turn, each with an *idée fixe*. Arising out of totally one-sided demands of the time (fortifications), their concepts result later, under different authors, in fantasies of baroque ornament, and the result becomes sterile, divorced from life, utopian; from a human viewpoint often less interesting than the worst "nonarchitectural city" à la Harbin or something similar. Not one of these purely ornamental ideal cities has been built.

One's thoughts are easily led from these straitjacketed schemes to city planning as presently practiced, which undeniably suffers in many ways from the psychology of the unfeasible ornamental plan. There exists at the moment an acute conflict between the city plan with its resultant codes and a building that follows contemporary developments. The more the city plan is based on the idea of the city as an aesthetic whole, the more difficult the conflict. The building up of an old master plan as a process can be seen essentially as a tearing down piece by piece of a formal system, where convulsive effort, however, is constantly expended to preserve an exterior appearance. The result is called a inified facade treatment when appearances fail less badly than usual. Often the conflict is worst when the building is an apartment house. One can, however, say with reason that zoning rules that allow a high density on a relatively small lot and limit design with the unified cityscape as the dominating aesthetic dogma, have the most damaging effect on buildings where light, sanitation, rational economics, and social considerations are of primary importance.

Finland has during the last four years seen a raging housing boom, followed now by a complete lull. Such is the world. But the recent building boom evokes certain thoughts in that it resulted for the most part in the building up of old (partly developed) previously planned areas of the city. An overwhelming majority of the new construction has been privately built apartment houses in the cen-

3

ters or their immediate surroundings, built according to existing master plans and zoning.

Helsinki has among other things gotten a whole city quarter finished during this period—the Töölö district adjacent to the center. The now finished district has, like so many European cities, classical roots inasmuch as it is, like the archeologist's Troy, really seven cities on top of each other—*in the city's planning archive.* The streets are laid out according to a compromise between the romantic Rothenberg plan from the turn of the century and a more classical plan of the same period, followed by many updated plans and finally a praiseworthy but frantic effort in the middle of the worst building fever to create a unified cityscape with the help of regulations governing facade materials and cornice lines, and roof slopes, heights, and materials. On the other hand, putting superficial aesthetic effects aside, efforts have been lacking to achieve more fundamental reforms in the utilization of the district's building lots, despite the fact that initially most of them belonged to the city. The result has become a hopeless housing canyon, where the small satisfaction derived from the fact that a few buildings use the same materials or window heights and cornice lines seems like wasted work and doesn't succeed in covering up the lack of a more humane and dignified grouping of houses. The idea accepted just about everywhere, that the completion of a partly developed district should have as its main consideration a superficial totality and stylistic unity with the previously built part, needs revision. In the case of Töölö, at the beginning of the building boom there were some half-built-up streets along with a large number of vacant, still unsold blocks. In such cases, if preconceived architectural viewpoints are set aside, it should be possible to carry out new construction based on more rational planning principles. The unified cityscape, the product of a forced formalism, involves a denial of progress. The achievement of a superficial unity where it essentially should not exist should gladden not one right-thinking soul.

The building up of older city quarters is a difficult problem everywhere: "The harmonious city" hangs like a sword suspended over each new piece of construction. The question has especially important implications in Finland because of the earlier widespread wooden buildings, which now one by one are being replaced by fireproof multistory blocks. In the medium-sized Finnish towns there are still a great number of wooden buildings in old areas bordering the city center. Since, according to the zoning laws, these lots have a right to six to ten times higher densities than those represented by the existing wooden buildings, these semicentral areas of town represent such a large opportunity for increasing available housing that it to a great extent undermines a healthy development of new areas on the periphery, where better housing conditions eventually could be achieved. Thus, in reality, housing construction takes place on these old building lots. It is therefore of great importance to try to achieve better housing on these lots than that which is supported by the rules and regulations that the zoning and building codes prescribe. I have already pointed out the missed opportunity in the case of Töölö. Similar missed opportunities are to be noted in other Finnish towns, most often in areas of privately owned wooden houses, where reform, therefore, is more difficult.

This problem naturally has greater relevance for Nordic cities, especially for the Finnish Empire-style town plans, somewhat Russian influenced in breadth and size. But in a large number of European cities new housing is built in partly developed areas or in place of old buildings that are torn down. This increase in available housing is significant enough so that there is reason to discuss how reform can be achieved so that construction follows improved ground rules.

When the problem is the completion of a partly developed city quarter, with groups of lots still unsold, the question of reform is easiest. Then the main obstacle is usually exterior aesthetic considerations, the desire to create a unified "city quarter." The architect should at that point break with the formal continuity of the older buildings and rearrange his buildings' orientation and other characteristics to take into primary consideration the desired changes in the buildings themselves. Where a road network already exists the new buildings should not have to line the street and "form facades." This does not under any circumstances have to result in the destruction of aesthetic values. The often-quoted adage that "consideration for existing buildings is a question of tact, not one of style," cannot often enough be repeated. The architect who does not use the word *style* as a stick-on label, a medium for creating *die Idealstadt*, but rather sees the production of housing as an extremely responsible social task, will find the right rhythm vis-à-vis the city as a growing organism. The regulation of private lots becomes a considerably more difficult question. Up to the maximum density for any lot, each cubic meter represents a capital value, and as most older zoning laws allow high densities, it becomes very difficult to achieve improvements without circumventing the lot owner's legal rights.

It would hardly be possible for the community in some way to buy back part of the building rights except in a crisis or through confiscatory legislation. We are left with the possibility of trying to achieve reform without reducing the allowable density of the lot. I know of only one case where a realistic proposal for systematic implementation has been suggested. The city planning office of Turku has worked out a proposal whose purpose is to prescribe a totally new way of building in the quarters covered by the old town plan (an extensive area with wooden houses). The buildings on each lot stand as separate entities with narrow (eighteen-meter) garden and service yards in the middle. A continuous facade is achieved, and the building's freestanding location makes possible an easier connection to utilities and services as they become available.

The allowable density has more or less been maintained while the houses have access to better natural light and a guaranteed relationship to their neighbors. From a rational building viewpoint the square building blocks represent, it is true, a fairly minimal improvement on the ordinary apartment construction on the blocks. Their point of departure is probably also partly formal (during the transitional period from wooden city to stone city, the half-

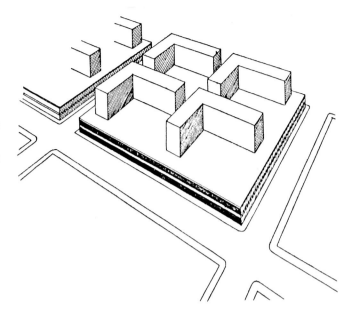

finished town type with exposed party walls etc. does not appear), but it has a solid foundation in its economic feasibility.

This same economy can be put to use even if we go to an even more rational solution. In other words, while maintaining allowable densities we allow a freestanding building that is sited and designed without preconceived notions, and that takes into consideration the demands of good living conditions, rather than having as its main task the forming of facades.

The formal city plan's inclination to divide up the city into center and periphery and as a result apply a formal discipline primarily to the center is often a sterile and unrealistic compositional device. One doesn't have to be especially sharp-eyed to discover that, especially in medium-sized towns, a large number of buildings are built so that a part of the house (the lower floor) has center functions (stores, garages, movies, workshops) and another part (the upper floors) is housing. *In other words, center and residential areas are mixed.* I include a sketch where the consequence is represented as *two cities on top of each other.* It has been done with consideration for the technical freedom which the development of the Turku plan should lead to. It is here included as a schematic sketch for the construction of business center block types, with existing needs as the point of departure. I am fully conscious of the difficulties that a transition from zoning with formal rules to building design according to practical needs brings with it and of the great limitations that have to be recognized. That there exist, however, many possibilities for rewarding work in this direction is clear. But it requires a thorough-going study of existing needs instead of formal, ideal-city projects, a rejection of the architect's old, implicit faith in the city as a plastic unity, a development of the art of city planning into what common sense tells us it should be— an elastic system for orchestrating the city's growth in all its different forms.

Byggmästaren, 1930

1. Innsbruck. From a trip to Italy, 1924

2. Old man. From a trip to Italy, 1924

8

3. Scrovegni Chapel, Padua, 1924

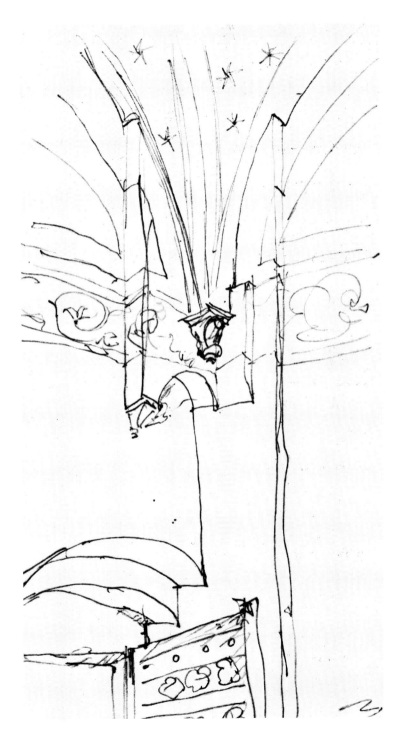

4. St. Mark's, Venice, 1924

10

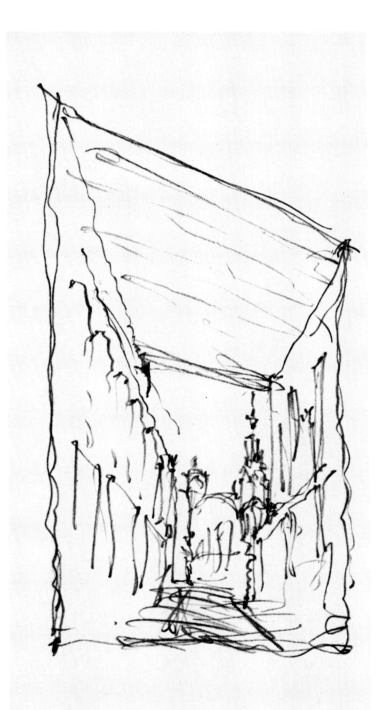

6. Trees, Delphi, 1953

12

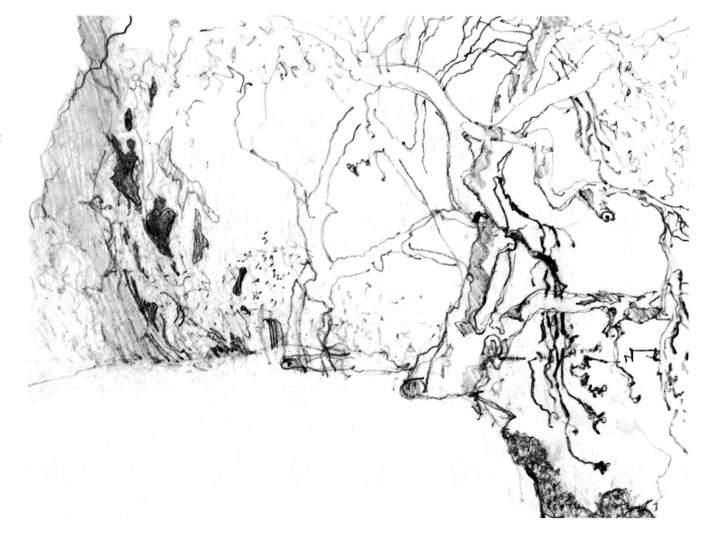

8. Temple of Apollo, 1953

14

The Stockholm Exhibition I

When I attended the Stockholm Exhibition's official opening I did not come as a stranger to see something new. I have to a great extent followed the exhibition organizers' work from the setting up of the first guidelines to the finished results. I therefore walked around and looked at it as a "friend of the exhibition," not as a temporary admirer but as one whose relationship to the object lies on a deeper plane.

The exhibition has, from its inception, been accompanied by an angry critique, with voices both for and against it. These voices have been raised as far away as our side of the Gulf of Bothnia. Not even when confronted by the results has the criticism died out; rather, it has increased in acerbity. Typical is Carl G. Laurin's judgment: "The best thing about the exhibition is that it is being torn down in the fall." A report card to which Albert Engstrom added further witticisms. One has to understand that the exhibition has even aroused some very harsh criticism since, after all, it applies a scalpel to the deeply entrenched inclination to link the concept of art with an elegant lifestyle and custom-made objects.

What most of the slanderers couldn't reason out for themselves is that the continuation of this antagonism between art and nonart results in greater and greater dissonance in society and leads to a life denial that is almost comic. But despite all the criticism there exist in Sweden excellent conditions for a change. I am thinking of all the social esprit, the industrial development, and of the positive attitude among intellectual circles. Therefore I believe that we are at the beginning of something new.

The exhibition speaks of a happy and relaxed daily life. It propagandizes consistently for a healthy and unaffected lifestyle based on economic realities. One might use a surgical metaphor and say that the appendix, where people's demands for luxuries and affected superficiality are housed, has been removed here. It is the desire for luxury that, under special circumstances, has been the point of departure for "artistic homes" but among a wider circle has resulted in silent tragedies: factory-made antique furniture and misguided values in the same vein. The Stockholm Exhibition wants to make manifest the modern artist's desire to create things for our present needs and for acceptable life values in accordance with the gains that the Swedish society has made.

The exhibition is organized so that in the first section one becomes acquainted with what Swedish industry has created in terms of cheap, usable objects for everyday life and in a second we can see how these typical industrial goods should be used within the home. In addition there is the home, which is presented in a series of experimental flats and houses. These dwellings have been built on tight budgets and use industrial methods of production.

We see an exhibition which in every way is socially oriented and aims at leveling the concept of art. Motorboats, buses, trains, refrigerators, and record players have been juxtaposed with what in times past was regarded as belonging to a higher plane and was called the noble art of interior design. All these new objects now appear with the same pretentions to being taken as cultural artifacts. It means that the design industry's creators are dropping their earlier attitude and stepping down from their assumed height to work in all domains and give form to all articles that are included among life's necessities. I see it as a very positive manifestation that the artist is in a sense denying himself by going outside of his traditional sphere of work, that he is democratizing his production and bringing it out of a narrow circle to a wider public. The artist thus steps in among the people to help create a harmonious existence with the help of his intuitive sensibility, instead of obstinately upholding the conflict between art and nonart which leads to acute tragedies and a hopeless life.

The biased social manifestation which the Stockholm Exhibition wants to be has been clad in an architectural language of pure and unconstrained joy. There is a festive refinement but also a childish lack of restraint to the whole. Asplund's architecture explodes all the boundaries. The purpose is a celebration with no preconceived notions as to whether it should be achieved with architectural or other means. It is not a composition in stone, glass, and steel, as the functionalist-hating exhibition visitor might imagine,

but rather a composition in houses, flags, searchlights, flowers, fireworks, happy people, and clean tablecloths. For Asplund, the Finnish tourist who rides the watercycle for one crown on Djurgården bay is a valuable object who gives the exhibition life. The surprise fireworks are part of the exhibition with the same justification as the exhibition showcases. He who criticizes the exhibition architecture only from the point of view of axes and facade angles will never, whether in his little ego he arrives at a positive or negative judgment, discover the mentality that has been the driving force behind the enterprise.

And for me, as "a friend of the exhibition," it is a great satisfaction that Gunnar Asplund, with this "denial of architecture," has hit the target and shown others to a way of thinking which hasn't previously led architecture to any triumphs. Even the gentleman who is used to finding satisfaction in traditional architectural beauty, where historical study and a good cultural drill have helped him get oriented, will perhaps gradually find reason for a whole new kind of joy as he walks around the Stockholm exhibition, where, for instance, blooming tulips in the garden have received the same care from the architects as the buildings and the exhibition hall interiors.

If the exteriors of the halls are the happy life without a damper, the interior is a total contrast, calm and coolly to the point. The exterior is a gala summer festival; the interior exhorts the visitor to look and think.

A better architectural exhibition principle than the one carried out here can hardly be found. The exhibition program prescribed from the beginning that the selection of exhibited objects would be made by the director of the exhibition, a decision which has led to superb results. One concludes that the mounting is so masterful that it often surpasses the objects on display. I have seldom seen an exhibition where the architecture has so totally had its point of departure in the psychology of viewing; in good lighting, good distinctions between the different groupings, and good traffic flow. When I say that the objects are not always on the same high level as the display, this does not imply criticism, as one of the exhibition's main principles is exactly the recognition of the need for improvement. The type of objects which have been created today will return next time with different characteristics.

A part of the exhibition's value lies in just the fact that the cooperation between industry and creativity, which was organized specially for the exhibition, is to continue even after it is over, with the goal of creating objects with a truer worth through cooperation. The Stockholm Exhibition will not end when it is dismantled this fall and Dr. Laurin gets his Djurgården back; it will continue in the form of an increased interaction between the parties mentioned. Life's immediacy will vouch for it, as a whole phalanx of good artists like to say.

In fact, much remains to be developed and improved upon. There were many objects which had more to them of overcomplicated style than of a natural solution. "The curl on the artistic tail has been straightened out, but it is for all that the same damn tail," said a Stockholm critic, who resolutely suggests that it be cut off.

The exhibition has put particular weight on the housing section, where the use of the wares is illustrated. Modern man, who with few exceptions should reflect on his housing problem, can here see and learn to value the gains architecture had made by setting itself the goal of being a social factor instead of, as earlier, dedicating too much attention to decorative and representational viewpoints. But it is important for the exhibition visitor not only to see but also to pay attention to the economic factors which have imposed upon the architects—Markelius, Åhren, and Almquist—a self-chosen limitation, which gives the results true value.

Comparisons have been made to former exhibitions in Stockholm. In them, however, mercantile Sweden played the key role. Here it is a question of intellectual Sweden's grasp on the average Swede—a sympathetic and understanding grasp which aims at removing his luxury appendix, an operation that the average Finn also needs.

Summary of an interview in *Åbo Underrättelser*, May 22, 1930

The Stockholm Exhibition II

"We have discovered that functionalist architecture is perfectly suited to exhibitions." This American statement is a striking proof of the conception that exhibitions are false architecture. The more the center of gravity within architecture is displaced from valuing individual synthesis, monuments, etc., toward a more organizational conception of relevant problems, the more meaningful becomes what we call an "exhibition," where one can introduce systems, methods, details, possibilities for development, and so on. Exhibitions can become, and must become, schools of social polemics that teach us how life's technical potential can be used properly. Thus they are very important elements in our cultural development. (In this regard exhibitions as catalysts to development surpass Wadstena Castle.) They are also a meaningful form of architecture; more meaningful than many other types, because the way in which these schools for the public are organized is of great importance. The Stockholm Exhibition is a school—a good school—and one cannot apply to it the criteria just mentioned, for judging "exhibition architecture."

The exhibition director defined the exhibition's scope roughly as architecture, building details, streets, gardens, methods of transport, and homes. It is remarkable that anyone could, in Sweden, arrange an exhibition according to such a clearly defined program. But it is not only the clear decision on a difficult question, "What shall be included and what not?" that pleases us. The dualism of mass-produced objects and prefabricated homes versus the individual house and the city outside is also to the point.

First the cars. Volvo's exterior did not promise a great deal; with its curved, "spare tire" architecture it would fit well in a comic strip. Then came the buses (Sundahl's bus was a Columbus egg), the boats, transport accessories, and a sports arena. Before looking at the standardized wares one would benefit from a brief visit to the planetarium, whose 27,000 years should be able to destroy the belief in the Empire style as our culture's firm foundation. In between visits to the exhibition of standardized wares we flirt a bit with fashion window displays, match and cigar kiosks (it is nice to have a cigar, just like a book, in a fine leather cover). The passage into the halls past the lighthearted kiosks was good architecture; it freed the visitor from the very solemn ceremony of the design object exhibit and made clear, for a simple individual, vanity's true value. Everywhere one meets the same protest against onesidedness and monument-worship. This is one of the Stockholm Exhibition's great values.

The standardized objects as such are obvious things that one expects to see, as also many that through exterior simplification have been made "modern" but whose justification in our society and true value can be questioned but for our familiarity with the idea of birthday gifts, something that the advertisements for Örrefors are also quite aware of. Glass and porcelain—naturally they include good things, but they are still too solidly anchored to the world-famous Swedish design industry. Among the suitcases one feels more at home. A bag with Lufthansa's colorful logo is somehow closer to the heart than the crystal we receive on our fiftieth birthday.

In the coffeepot department an intelligent person can find a good coffeepot, and in the same way each division of standardized wares has its good things. If one looks at these wares in a totally different context—as articles created mainly to satisfy varied taste, which according to the manufacturers exists among the general public (and because the manufacturers think it "fun" to create many different types)—then one is inclined to see both the good and the bad in the whole collection as pedagogically correct. The person who wanders around here will, without being conscious of it, learn something about life in relationship to the practical properties of his possessions. Here he will guess that his relationship with countless "tasteful objects" is a pattern he will outgrow, and that the satisfaction of owning an original object of "one's very own" is nothing compared to the joy provided by an honest, functioning utility article—the same one the neighbors have.

That so-called individual taste receives a shove in the right direction from the architecture of the exhibition. From the mania for collecting mahogany and crystal the soul will eventually develop so that it acquires the capacity and the imagination to appreciate the values of the moment— fresh flowers, a bright tablecloth, good coffee.

The ultimate worth of the fine manner in which Asplund has succeeded in making the exhibition a happy folk festival is the cultural-political orientation already mentioned. Parallel to the organization of housing this orientation is particularly valuable for humanity. In a charming form it embraces a deeply serious "propaganda" for man's innermost life instincts.

Against this background I would like to say that the Stockholm Exhibition is not only good but also effective.

Many a despiser of functionalism is surely walking around at this very moment as an unwitting "carrier".

The minimal dwelling isn't an independent product like the manor house of times past. It absolutely demands its counterpart in the wider collective architecture. The smaller the home is, the more daily functions are moved over to common facilities. The fact has perhaps not been made clear enough at the exhibition. But an exhibition technique that would illuminate the problem is hard to achieve, and the relationship has after all been clearly pointed out. The Stockholm Exhibition is the first one in the world where one has consciously presented this problem.

The housing exhibition's strength, its plus, lies in the fact that, as an organizational whole, it strives to be and is an institution, insofar as exact scientific analysis of the housing problem has led to a series of studio solutions, freely constructed by various talents, but with a common point of departure, so that comparisons, calculations, and critiques can be systematized.

As an experience, with a relationship to the problem in its whole width, an exhibition of this type is more positive than if it had had a direct anchoring in reality, in other words, if it had been part of some model housing quarter in Stockholm. Exhibitions of the latter type can clearly be useful as well as give us a practical overview, but they do not provide an equally comprehensive range for speculation.

The housing exhibition's weakness is that it is so heterogeneous and that healthy radicalism has partly been left out or has become radical in the bad (artistic) meaning of the word.

The general organization is sound, the best possible, and the whole exhibition shows clearly that precisely the organization, the mounting of the exhibition, and the clarification of trends are on a higher level than most of the objects. In other words, the level is very high. The overall quality of the objects is, however, also quite good. But here in these model dwellings one could have used the conjectural totality more effectively. It could have been more like a precise housing study without putting its main emphasis on immediately achieving a ready-made comfortable home.

In most cases the standard is quite good. The point of departure is right, thanks to the high level of organization already mentioned, but the results are more meager—the furniture, its grouping, the lighting, etc., has often not risen above cliché standards of comfort. The shortcut that would immediately create a "comfortable" home has in many cases become an obstacle which has put a stop to the precise study, the "each article by itself analysis" of different floor plans and details, which remain totally wrapped in obscurity. Seen in the context of the total effect the work of the more radical architects appears very significant.

It requires radicalism to avoid creating a superficial comfort and instead to search out the problems whose solution could create the conditions for better architectural work and achieve truly usable criteria for people's well-being in their everyday lives. Such a method of working can be bold enough to display ostentatiously a half-finished object when the conditions are lacking (at low enough cost) to make it attractive to the eye. This does not have to mean bad material for the viewing public, as one can conclude from the radical creations at the Stockholm Exhibition. There is a great deal of balanced radicalism in the housing exhibition, especially in the work of Markelius and Åhren, but also in that of others. In comparison to artistic radicalism, a very common article on the world market, this radicalism gains from the point of view that it is not destroyed by the law of action and reaction; it evolves.

The Danish magazine *Kritisk Revy* once published a picture of Tivoli: paper lanterns in the leafy branches above a cafe table. The heading was "Eternal Values." The Stockholm Exhibition has the same kind of eternal values in its whole exterior articulation. "There is not one exhibition that rivals this one in its total effect," said Sigfried Giedion to the author. "I regard Weissenhof as historically more significant, yes, and a few Werkbund exhibitions, but Stockholm. . . ." I agree.

"Tukholman näyttely II," *Arkkitehti*, 1930

20

9. Theater, Delphi, 1953

10. Donkey, Delphi, 1953

22

13. Trees and ruins, Olympia, 1953

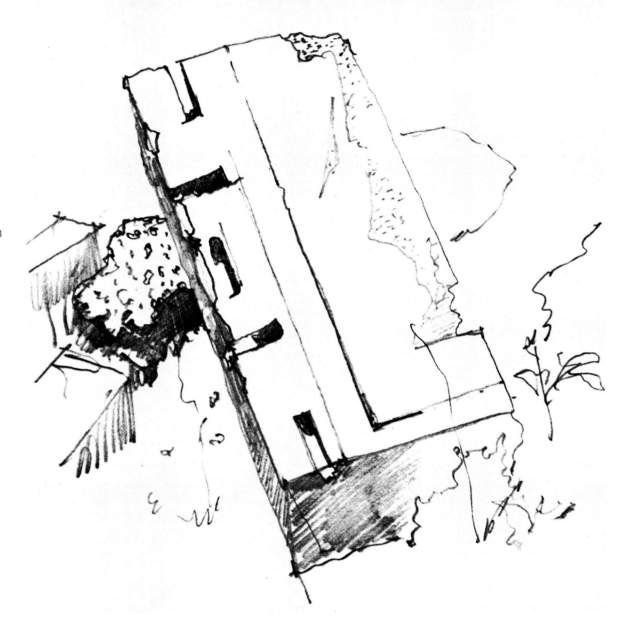

The Dwelling as a Problem

Words that are used in different situations by different people of different social classes can often express very different concepts. Sometimes they are given directly opposite meanings.

The concept "room" exists in a final "proletarianized" form but continues to have the same meaning it had in the palaces from which it is a descendant. The living room in a peasant farmhouse—whose Finnish name *tupa* developed from the Lapp *kota*, in Swedish *kata*—is a combination of different functions and was never, before its period of decline, combined with the concept "room."

In the city dwelling, on the other hand, the room continues to exist in an artificial manner, as an inheritance from palace architecture, in circumstances where it is really no longer appropriate. No family can live in one room, not even two, if they have children. But any family can live on an equivalent area if this area is divided up with particular attention to this family and its members' lives and activities. A dwelling is an area which should offer protected areas for meals, sleep, work, and play. These biodynamic functions should be taken as points of departure for the dwelling's internal division, not any outdated symmetrical axis or "standard room" dictated by the facade architecture.

Modern man—and the family—are more mobile than before. This is reflected in furniture's mechanical characteristics. Sixty square meters—and morning exercise for the whole family: this assumes that the furniture can be easily moved and folded up.

There are large, 200-square-meter apartments where morning exercise becomes almost comically impossible, to say the least, in among heavy cupboards, symmetrically placed tables, undisturbable monumental masses, and diverse fragile decorative glass.

On the other hand, moveable and foldable furniture enlarge a minimal dwelling. And in fact, the whole method of designing the interior that I have mentioned aims at enlarging the dwelling by developing its use possibilities.

In and of themselves, large dimensions are no advantage, but rather a drawback. If we take a minimal dwelling as our point of departure and strive to increase the use possibilities for its various parts with the purpose of psychologically making the dwelling appear roomier, then we arrive at a concept, no longer of a minimal dwelling, but of a universal dwelling—a dwelling which in its characteristics is better and more correct than the one where an emotional handling of the spaces has led to an unorganic totality.

There will come a time when we will happily trade a dwelling of 250 square meters for one of 70 square meters—and the time is close.

What housewife wants a large kitchen these days? A wise housewife wants a kitchen which is easy to work in, in other words, a kitchen where all unnecessary space has been eliminated. In addition, psychological factors must be taken into consideration. Among them one can perhaps count the so-called "sense of well-being." Of this concept, which is relatively undefined, one can say that it is a product of many different factors.

But we can perhaps claim that a dwelling where shifts, movements, changes from one activity to another can happen organically, without bother and interruptions, and where certain special measures have been taken to achieve pleasant acoustics and proper light, represents a high standard of well-being.

People's predilection to surround themselves with a special world of forms, be it however primitive, has often been brought up in protest against housing construction and interior design of dwellings based on mass production. Question: these dwellings produced for profit which aspire only to present taste, with Empire-style imitations, or the interior decorating business, which does public relations for all types of unusable status furniture, factory baroque, etc., at cheap prices—do they create the perfect conditions for the free individual?

That free individual appears for the most part as a product of so many coincidences that it can hardly be dealt with in a scientific manner in conjunction with technical production. One thing is clear: research based on human similarities, which is what lies as the basis of the scientifically involved dwelling concept, does not violate the hypothetical free individual. One can actually take along one's own distinct personality to the new dwelling as a portable belonging.

On the other hand, what was earlier considered developed taste and found its expression in the collecting of objects, in owning things and in feeling a heavy inheritance responsibility, is often transformed these days into a characteristic which I experience as a more human cultural value. It becomes a lovely, almost intellectual ability to grasp and enjoy the moment's and brief instant's *values*.

Therefore a few words about what I mean in this context by the word *values*, emotional and aesthetic, economic and social. I have participated in long discussions about culture versus civilization, I have heard these words mentioned in all types of contexts. It is possible that the concept "culture" cannot be defined in a short sentence. Therefore I will use an example. An ocean liner. In the engineer's cabin by the writing table sits the engineer, who supervises the boat's turbine engines. On the wall, automatic measuring instruments tick away, producing diagrams and information on fuel consumption, steam pressure, revolutions per minute, temperatures, etc. Together this milieu and the man in it form a typical totality of organic work. It is likely that the man in question is more or less indifferent to whether the bunk in his cabin is of one type or another or if the walls are according to the latest style or not. In contrast he does value unaffected comfort, a restful atmosphere, and a good book when he has time and he reacts, one assumes, with a certain warmth to the organic whole of which he himself, his writing, his rest, and his automatic turbines are elements. I do not mean by the word *culture* any machine symbolism but rather the balanced mentality generated by work, organization, and an uncomplicated everyday life in which irrelevant elements essentially appear silly. It is this mentality I call culture.

On the upper deck aboard the same ship is Lady Astor with lady in waiting and retinue on her way home from Paris. In Paris she has learned the names of ten new cocktails. She knows that they are wearing lamé and the fur of a certain type of fox this season, she has heard lectures about Pascal, Victor Hugo, and Montespan, she has played tennis with Duke Miesojenoff and for the first time visited the Faubourg St. Germain. I do not regard tennis as something noncultural but the totality formed by Lady Astor's luxury suite with Empire-style bed, fashionable wallpaper, and cocktail-Victor Hugo-Montespan culture is fairly exactly what I would like to call nonculture. And on the other hand to get an additional perspective on this totality in first class I want to say that I regard as culture that milieu and mentality which is represented by a modern working woman whose interest in literature is not a sensational selection and whose habits and possessions have an organic relationship with her work and life's responsibilities. In that milieu one can of course also drink and play tennis, but all this can nonetheless serve as an example of what I mean by culture.

By the words *aesthetic* and *emotional* I do not mean any lack of a sense of beauty or feeling, but an activity and attitude which takes certain schematic, inculcated concepts of beauty and expressions of feeling from the past as the point of departure instead of seeing them in the context of their proper historic connection, as once upon a time the result of an organic development.

By the word *economic* I do not mean the kind of economy that at one time was the practice in the American Pullman company's trains. They were said to be practical and economical trains, but a wise traveler always observed that their practical and economical aspects worked to the Pullman company's advantage, not the passengers'.

Why in fact do we use the word *problem* in referring to modern man's dwelling? Things become problems when all the factors that originally influenced them have changed. Despite the fact that one has gotten used to looking at the dwelling problem quite traditionally and only certain periods of housing shortages and certain questions of price sometimes appear problematic, we must note (if we deal with the problem scientifically) that most of the factors that constitute the basic premises for our dwelling have changed in recent times. It is unnecessary to list here all the social changes that have been brought about by the natural sciences and industry. Let us merely note in short that a society based on prestige and clearly etched class distinctions belongs to the past.

Now that such distinctions are almost eliminated and the cross section of society is different, what are the factors and motives that are decisive for the housing question? We are still living partly in a period of transition from old to new. When we try to list the basic requirements of the housing question we cannot avoid at the same time comparing present norms with those of the past.

The only possible factors and motives with which one can replace the old criteria are scientific studies of what people and society unconditionally need in order to remain, or better yet, to develop into, a healthy organism.

Even during its primitive history the dwelling had certain primary biological functions that still exist. Everyone must live somewhere.

To arrive at difficult conclusions some sciences use a method of analyzing, not a normal case, but one that in one way or another is extreme. When we set out to examine man's dwelling we cannot find norms other than minimal ones, and these we have to seek out among special cases, in other words, they are geared to a dwelling built for the minimum borderline of human needs. A luxury house, a large dwelling, cannot involve any problems, but in minimal dwellings everything becomes a problem. The minimal dwelling is also an appropriate object of study because it represents the concept of economy and what comes to be most people's lot. Only in this manner can we get at the scientific conditions for the standard dwelling in society, that which in the name of rationalism should approximate a clearly understood minimum.

Every individual is energy, and from a social point of view to manage this energy badly involves waste of the greatest sort. It is meaningless to examine the worst conditions in which an individual can remain alive. We have certainly had enough examples of such a minimal line. What we will examine here is the question of what demands should be placed on the dwelling, on the production and consumption of dwellings so that they will (on the subsistence borderline) meet the demands of social positivism.

The biological conditions for human life are, among others, air, light, and sun. Air does not have to do with the size of the rooms or their number. It is an independent concept. We can surely build a dwelling with a large cubic footage of air without using the floor area uneconomically and affecting the ceiling height. The air space is a question of ventilation. On the other hand one must give a great deal of consideration to the air's quality. And this is a question that is dependent on the city's internal organization, the town plan.

Light and sun. Under extreme conditions one can no longer leave the dwelling's access to the sun to chance. Light and air are such important preconditions for living that the haphazard conditions that prevail today must be changed. The norms should not only require that each dwelling get sun; the angle of incidence should also be decided, to, let us say, one degree's leeway. The sun is a source of energy; but only if we use it in a scientific way and in exact quantities will it become, under all circumstances, a positive factor for the biodynamic concept that involves the family's and the single individual's life within the dwelling's walls. In a fifty-square-meter dwelling we don't have, in this regard, the slightest margin to be left to chance, nor can we afford to allow the sun's and the light's energy to remain unused. And at the same time we have to eliminate the inconveniences that these same factors, under unfavorable circumstances, can lead to.

What then are the forces that stand in the way of progress? As everyone knows, the modern city is governed by chance as far as orientation is concerned. Statistics on dwellings in Helsinki would show that they can be divided into groups of approximately the same size, which point in all directions of the compass. The city in our day represents, even when it is claimed to be subject to the most modern development, only a clumsy and inorganic development phase, behind which the old asocial, prestige-ori-

ented city continues to live and to dominate the minds of the planners. Our city planning involves a misguided admiration for the past based on sentimental and affected aesthetic motives. The belief in some type of absolute and definitive architectural laws is an obstacle to the organic concept of the city. Emotional conservatism has been given a prominent role in the town planning task. Just a small observation: each building is built according to the zoning codes so that it is in accordance with the established architectural scheme, harmonizes with existing buildings. It should be pointed out that neither medical science nor any other natural science accepts an equivalent technical archaism.

Most families in Helsinki own nothing but a percentage of a paved courtyard beyond the walls of their own apartment. And yet the normal dwelling concept, with its minimal standards, includes the possibility of having at one's disposal an exterior space that should be regarded as part of the home. This is also a town planning question but does not in itself presuppose any kind of sentimental, garden-city type of thinking, which must be rejected because, among other reasons, it becomes uneconomical. Each dwelling should technically be constructed so that it includes a usable outdoor space which biologically is equivalent to the nature man was accustomed to before the large cities developed. We can actually go so far (and it is perhaps the right way to go) as to make the outdoor spaces collective, in other words, common for a certain group of dwellings. The fact that this space is partly conceived for children and child care in an age when it is usual for the mother to have a regular job indicates that a common solution is desirable.

In a time when both government funds and million-dollar donations are building institutes whose task is to discover one single bacterium, publishers are still publishing an enormous mass of books on sentimental interior decorating, rya weaving, tapestry copies, chair and sofa styles, etc. Only one book is still unpublished in this world; the one on the physiological dwelling.

Which would the scientifically definable needs be, those that could for physiological or other reasons be regarded as norms for the dwelling's interior layout and equipment?

Most people look at the room as a standard measure for the dwelling. In big dwellings there are many rooms and a kitchen. If we descend the ladder we finally arrive at the classical Helsinki miniature dwelling, "room with stove."

In addition to those already mentioned, additional changes have taken place in the relationship that determine the dwelling's internal arrangement. Up to our day, society has been more or less paternalistic. Seen as a group, we humans are strange animals. During an era when we are in certain respects taken care of according to scientific and rational principles, one can at the same time in a group of people find individuals who appear not to have changed since feudal times, and even antiquated forms of activity and ways of thinking, which no doubt were fully motivated during man's nomadic period. One circumstance that to a great extent has influenced the patriarchal family life traces its origin to the same period as the previously mentioned major changes. This is the total transformation of women's role in our times.

Her emancipation and subsequent rise from a subordinate position both in working life and in the home to become an equal work companion places totally new demands on the dwelling. And with this change come others, which might be collectively described as a decentralization of family life.

The dwelling is no longer built as a totality for a patriarchal family. In the past it was the relatives' duty to take care of widows and children; still earlier a man would marry his dead brother's widow. These days the family continues to exist even when such events occur. But these two entities, a complete family and only mother and children are different in terms of living conditions and requirements. This demands of our housing production an ability to adapt which previously hadn't been necessary, because one must regard it as highly asocial if the dwelling cannot offer one of these groups the same possibilities as the other. Even if a fatherless family is regarded as an exception that housing production need not take into consideration, one can on the other hand point out that even changes in our concept of sexual roles, also a result of scientific development, naturally increases the number of families headed by a female.

The same decentralization phenomenon within the family places the following very important demands on the dwelling's internal divisions: each member of the family should be able to completely isolate himself within the dwelling's walls. Not even in this case can we operate with the concept of rooms; rather, we have to resort to half-rooms and a system where insulation (for instance in the bedroom) and common spaces become factors which no sentimental layout of room, no axial symmetry, can affect any longer. When a way of installing insulation must be created in a small area, 60 square meters, the question of sound insulation becomes especially important; just this might lead to the development of a requisite technology in, for instance, insulation tiles.

In this modern society it is possible, at least theoretically, for the father to be a mason, the mother a college professor, the daughter a film star, and the son something still worse. Obviously each would have special needs to be allowed to think and work undisturbed. The modern dwelling must be built in accordance with these needs.

In the same manner, women's emancipation leads to totally new demands on work conditions, such as easy cleaning and consideration of different utensils' weight and mechanical utility.

It is funny to observe how people in general primarily understand form as a fashion phenomenon, an aesthetic sensation; imagine, for example, metal tubing furniture that would actually be weightless and have increased mechanical possibilities. Different designs for chairs which have meant less wear on rugs, etc., have in many cases been treated as purely formal novelties.

"Asuntomme probleemina," *Domus*, 1930

33

Letter from Finland

1. Finland is an agrarian country even though these days farming is no longer profitable. What then is the state of the architecture of our countryside? I could show you quite a lot of well-built, solid farmhouses and barns, good from the point of view that old building methods have been followed, or ancient aesthetic concepts have been improved upon thanks to the "new technology." But the tasks have changed. The facts that agriculture is turning to cooperative operations, that the small villages are developing into regional centers, etc., put new tasks before us. But a building method organically developed to do these tasks, or a dominant method of organization, doesn't exist.

2. There is an abundance of lumber in Finland. All of our older architecture is based on handicraft-type wood building methods. Even today in large parts of the country it is most natural to build of wood and by hand. At a relatively early stage industrial standard building was introduced (Helsinki's garden suburbs). Almost without exception it has involved mechanical standardization of the type that, in American houses from before the World War, imitated old handicraft forms.

Now we are, however, in the process of converting from wood to fireproof building methods (in the larger cities the conversion had already occurred by 1900). Industrially produced building elements of wood, with all their possibilities for development, have up to now influenced building methods very little. Wood insulation, in conjunction with reinforced concrete, has for the most part merely been a valuable aid to traditional construction methods.

Here there continues to exist—as in other countries—a duality between technique and "art."

3. Urban architecture is essentially the same here as everywhere else and is dealt with in just as shallow a manner. Urban architecture in Finland has, however, certain special problems. The traditional phase between small town and big city is (though on a smaller scale) of course just as unplanned here as in other countries.

In the periphery of almost all cities exist inorganic new suburbs and hardly a single well-organized housing area. The "rental barracks" has, up to now, been the main dwelling unit in urban construction, and in lieu of any evolved principles of dwelling, it has unfortunately been treated as a monumental building. Exceptions to this rule are very few. Our urban architecture still has a long way to go from form playing on paper to a practical system capable of development.

4. Housing construction has up till now been quite pitiful despite the intensive building period of 1924–1929. Officially there is no shortage of housing, but the manner in which housing construction is carried on (presently we have a crisis and are building very little) can with reason be called pitiful. All the parts of the city that previously consisted of one-story wooden housing have become prime targets for real estate speculation while the cities are being transformed into "stone cities." Housing in Finland is a rental barracks industry, whether private or cooperative.

Even cooperative building can, in its present badly organized form, be seen as a kind of speculative activity. Financially, construction is misdirected because the motivating force is the developers' private economic interests, and architecturally it is misdirected because the point of departure is formalist and in the end it is the cost calculations that determine the size and execution of the unit.

To a certain extent building is carried on with the financial support of the community or the church; unfortunately this is also a fairly badly planned side activity that essentially lacks significance.

It is perhaps the badly planned building of "rental barracks" that is to blame for the fact that the design of housing is regarded as a type of inferior architecture. There are architects who, side by side with their urban and monumental projects, pursue a second-class art in their numerous speculative apartment buildings.

5. Urban building. If it is handsome buildings you want to see, then I have much to show you. Business palaces, skyscraper hotels, Scandinavia's largest department store, public buildings, etc. They may be traditional or "modern" but in one respect both groups are, in their striving for a personal monumentality, bound by tradition.

There exists very little architecture in which the only point of departure is human needs.

Building and town planning include, in other words, little architecture in the sense of organic building. Precisely the situation that exists in most of the rest of the world.

Instead of architecture I can only present problems. But problems aren't unfruitful. They will become the foundation for the true architectural school of our era. I can only refer to the struggle that is going on in the Finland of today around the search for an ideological, attitudinal, and technical basis for an organic architecture.

"Ein Brief von Finnland," *Bauwelt*, 25/1931

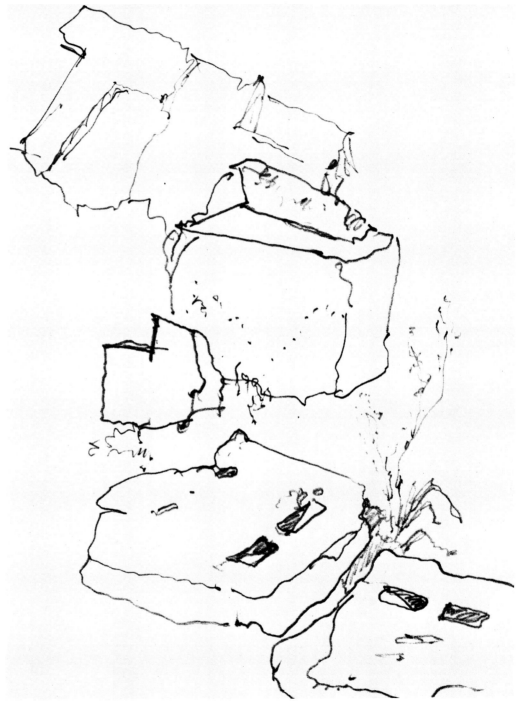

36

38

20. Windmills, Mykonos, 1953

39

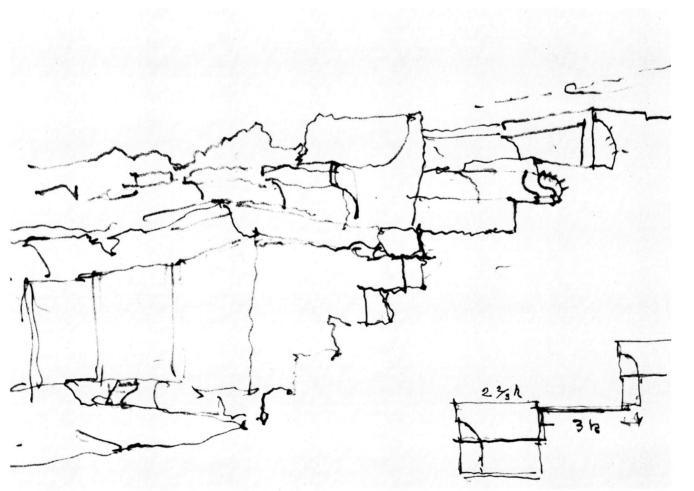

23. Pallastunturi, 1930s

42

The Geography of the Housing Question

The big city in its real form or as the embryo of what all population accumulation and concentration of production lead to is a direct product of industrialism. These close-to-absolute contrasts to the countryside are familiar to everyone, though few bother to investigate what the contrast really involves. In short, we have two forms of life, city and country—*A*-Europe and *B*-Europe they have been called—where most life functions have different practical solutions. Out of the condensed growth that has benefited *A* there has arisen a paradox typical of our planless culture, with a disorganizing effect on future development.

The following claim has often been made: Industrial development, the applied sciences, inventions, etc., do not imply only a tendency to concentration; one can always find in them even an opposite tendency—inventions that facilitate decentralized forms of housing; planning possibilities for traffic and public transportation; the reduction of distances through faster means of conveyance; improvement of personal contacts, despite distance, via telephone and radio.

The person who says this most often means something along the following lines: one should not take the contrast between countryside and city so tragically; each has its special faults, but essentially they complement each other. And that our present system should take the contrast to its ultimate absurdity is not conceivable. Industrialism has only in its infancy led to an unplanned concentration of population; in the future it will contain stabilizing forces; all new inventions ease human contacts in one way or another with the increasing independence of distances. The unsound and exaggerated aspects in the country-city dichotomy will work itself out, and a balance will ensue.

Pronouncements along this line are cause for an inquiry into the possibilities of resolving the "country-city" contrast. The question in its totality is not separable from other major questions of our time; its solution is one with theirs; but the generally held conception I have just described gives us the clear delimitation needed for such a short essay. To see the solution of the situation purely as a traffic problem is naturally too limited, but the need for contact between individuals and groups that exists in a deeper sense can be taken as a point of departure for a short and superficial study of the geography of the housing question. We can begin with the radio, the most popular and most typical "invention" among all technical gadgets that facilitate human communication. Is it really a force for decentralization? The winged phrase "the radio in the remote northern log cabin" points to a tendency in that direction. The purely mechanical possibility of an easily accessible contact between large masses of people that the radio clearly offers changes right away our conception of the large city and the intellectual need for people to cluster together. But soon one discovers the onesidedness; the log cabin is only a receiver; the city broadcasts. It means greater dependence for the periphery, for the countryside in relationship to the city. It is highly doubtful that the radio, even considering its perfectability, should be considered to bring with it a spontaneous readjustment in the contrast between country and city. There are better reasons to label it a strong centralizing force.

Telephone?

It is true that the telephone shortens the distance between Stockholm and Turku, Prague, and Paris. There it can be said to work for decentralization. But at shorter distances, as a direct line of communications within a province, it becomes something very different. The telephone, with its main trunks, local exchanges, and individual lines radiating from them is as close as possible in its organization to *nature's biological organization principles: communication between cells in local groupings*. There are no trees whose berries grow directly on the trunk; they are carefully grouped on smaller branches. The costs of the telephone, for wires, exchanges, and maintenance, do not favor a succinct one-to-one principle. A scattered, random, thinly populated area—the countryside—and the large city, cluttered beyond all reason—these are the clearly unplanned settlements. The economics of the telephone leads instead to an organic branching out of settlements; *it allows for geographic decentralization based on local groupings*.

If calculations based on the telephone were allowed to determine our housing setup, the country could become a system of scattered settlements similar in size and in a certain sense similar in character, but with no individual cells arbitrarily located.

The economics of the telephone is of course a minor matter in our overall national economy. But it shows with a funny, almost graphic, clarity, that can be seen in the overhead lines by every hobo, what the ideal conditions for settlements are when the need for contact between people is set as the criterion.

In such a study of the geography of the housing question the telephone can be taken as a kind of symbol for all other types of communication. It will become apparent that if the economies of roads and streets, the railroads, the telegraph, and the postal service's organizational principles were to be taken as the point of departure for the geographic location of housing, each one would encourage local groupings but not single cells. The distance between groupings would on the other hand not be of the same importance as their inner organization. We have already touched upon institutions that exist especially for a form of communication. They are in a certain sense mechanical objects, and the tendency in them is fairly clear. Before we turn to more central life functions it should be noted that even they, with modern methods of organization, are indirectly a part of human interaction. Schools and education, sanitation, and health care, division of production and foodstuff distribution, yes, in the end all types of production and raw materials acquisition can be so labeled.

For example, take the school. What is it but a distribution apparatus, an intellectual one, subject, like all such institutions, to the rule that it becomes most economical and functions most effectively in a milieu whose inner structure is specially suited for its rational use. A school cannot be organized satisfactorily in a sparsely populated countryside. It requires a greater density of dwellings around it. On the other hand, it can function to a certain extent just as well in Lapland as in Southern Europe provided that this local settlement exists and is properly constituted.

The school can be taken as a "textbook example" even for the other societal functions listed, which, to the extent that they involve distribution, consumption, etc., are al-

45

ways dependent on easy contact with a larger group of individuals.

The cells' tendency to group themselves (biology's principle of construction) will also confirm itself in this case, and it is easy to see that a study of all human needs and their rational satisfaction points to the absolute need for a settlement pattern with a fixed basic element, a fixed dwelling grouping, a societal unit. It would on the whole surprise me if in addition this basic element, if studied branch for branch—traffic, telephone, food distribution, etc.,—did not take the same dimensions, totally independent of the fact that the most suitable form of organization of, for example, the school, should be possible to implement in a community type, a housing group, which at the same time is the ideal norm for the means of communication. That industrial production makes the grouping of housing necessary is unquestionably clear. On the other hand, it is conceivable that different types of industries require housing groupings of very different sizes, primarily perhaps because different branches of production are not equally developed in terms of their degree of industrialization. An important leveling factor is industrialization itself, the replacement of human labor by machines, as well as the economic planning trends that regulate supply and demand. In addition there is the fact that the dimensions of the dwelling group will be kept so low that a large, concentrated industry will require many such groupings, in other words, a "group of groups." This is necessary simply in consideration of topographical conditions that can place a clear limit on a societal unit's dimensions. Housing construction itself, transformed into the industrial manufacture of standard elements and ready-made products, is a considerably more stable form of production than the handicraft type of building construction, with its large and often transient labor force. The gradual historic achievement of a comprehensive settlement pattern for the whole country, in the geographic sense, will also have its practical results in the stabilization of the backward construction industry. The production of building elements and interiors will be increasingly transferred to industries at fixed locations, while the labor force for construction becomes increasingly limited to something that paradoxically can be called assembly brigades.

I have said that the study of different life functions, used to define the most suitable type of standard housing groupings, would give fairly similar results. The following objection is raised to this idea: rural individualism is a direct consequence of the farmer's techniques. That is what caused the empty countryside and the cluttered city. This is correct. But it is correct only so long as farming has a technique that isn't as developed as other forms of production. When it has become so and the resources already exist, though society's present structure partly hinders their full use, then a study of the housing question for the agricultural sector will also point to the desirability of local dwelling groupings. And even here, the same inner structure of the unit as in the other cases, but with necessary adjustments, will show itself most suitable.

The reply to the general conception outlined at the beginning of this essay becomes, in other words: The contrast between countryside and city in its present form is, it is true, a transitional phase, but technology will not introduce a spontaneous shift in the sense that the growth of the cities at a certain moment would stop and the city and countryside would remain in their present form. Industrialism, technology, modern organization, have decentralizing tendencies solely if there is a meaningful local centralization.

The countryside's individualism will disappear, the exaggerated and planless in the city as well. Instead there should be a settlement pattern where only the increased density of fixed dwelling groups will remind one of the present large city.

The modern city planner's way of working primarily with the city district—the dwelling group—is a useful, pioneering technique that can be used as an element in geographic urbanization of the countryside—the inheritor of the old art of town planning.

Arkitektur och samhälle, 1932

Rationalism and Man

The situation within the applied arts today is not of the simplest kind; least of all should it be characterized by the opposing relationship, "traditional-modern."

A better picture in this case would be a three-sided conflict along the lines of *Kritisk Revy*'s traditionalism-modernism-realism. The two first mentioned are naturally form-and-feeling–oriented approaches; the third could even be called rationalism.

At the moment we live in an intoxication of modernism; the old resistance from the traditionalist side has grown weaker. In a way both groups have grown closer and together form a large formalist front that stands in opposition to a rational view of life and art. An accusation against rationalism from this front would perhaps be formulated in the following manner.

"The form of an object independent of its other properties and playing with form involve in and of themselves a universal human value of highest importance. Rational working methods certainly have their given place in the preliminary work. But to build up the applied arts based on rationalism as a cultural factor leads to inhumanity."

Let us examine the amount of truth in this rebuke. It can be imagined that the rebuke is fairly accurate. A confrontation with the mass of the *neue Sachlichkeit* produced in recent times causes a person to take a skeptical attitude and makes him ready to pursue loyally all criticism directed against it. One realizes, of course, that even the true rationalism, which has been created during the last ten years, may be lacking in many ways and often precisely vis-à-vis the concept of humanity, *but the question is how "free-form" formalism will become the savior*. Modern industrial design is a fairly good answer to this question. Modernism has, of course, essentially made its breakthrough not on its own but on rationalism's authority. Modernism has run amuck with the world of forms that has arisen through the analysis of materials, new working methods, new social conditions, etc., and made of it a pleasant compote of chromed tubes, glass tops, cubistic forms, and astounding color combinations. One has a feeling that here every effort has been made so that the new architecture would acquire happier, and, I assume, also more humane features, and yet it is something more like a depressing feeling of just this lack of the human element that grips one. The reason that this currently most conspicuous branch of the applied arts, formalism, succeeds so poorly in its appeal is partly, I suppose, that the inspiration for it has not to any great extent been human goals. Whatever the cause, the production of "form functionalism" has been enormous and in any case extensive enough to clarify the fact that mutual independence of form and function is not the way in which people will get better and more human things with which to build their surroundings.

We have conceded and we should be agreed upon the fact that objects that properly can be given the label *rational* often suffer from a noticeable lack of human qualities. If we disregard for a moment the possibility that the missing element can be introduced merely by adding "more form" and instead try to make a closer study of the facts, we soon come to the insight that *the rationality of the object most often applies to a few of its characteristics but not to all*. Originally rationalism meant something connected with the method of production. It is not certain that the first impetus for rational architecture was the production technique but it certainly was one of the first. If we think of a tubular metal chair, let us say one of Marcel Breuer's first models, we can clearly conclude: the impetus for its creation has its source in a series of interrelated desires to make pieces that would be lighter than before but just as comfortable and that, especially in their method of manufacture, are oriented to present-day methods of production. The finished product has above all received the imprint of the production method. To achieve a springy seat merely with a few bent tubes and some tightly stretched bits of leather is in itself a clever technical solution. It can in this regard justly be labeled rational. It can also be considered so in many other respects, primarily from a structural viewpoint. But a chair has an endless series of requirements that it should, when finished, fulfill and not till it fulfills all of them in a reasonable way, without different requirements coming into conflict with

each other, can it be regarded as a thoroughly rational creation. One can of course understand the word *rational* in a variety of ways, but the main criterion is fulfilling all the definable rational requirements so that they form a totality without conflict.

If we wish to list the requirements that these chairs do not succeed in filling we could mention the following: a piece of furniture that forms a part of a person's daily habitat should not cause excessive glare from light reflection; ditto, it should not be disadvantageous in terms of sound, sound absorption, etc. A piece that comes into the most intimate contact with man, as a chair does, shouldn't be constructed of materials that are excessively good conductors of heat. I merely name these three criteria that the tubular metal chairs hardly fulfill. One could list a large number of additional requirements that in this particular case are not met. The main criticism against the metal chairs has been that they are not what one would call "cozy." This has in most cases been true, but when one uses the concept of "coziness" to mean something totally, undefinably human and claims that only traditional formalism could create it then one is on the wrong path. The criticisms, too noisy, too light-reflective, and too good a heat conductor, *are in reality scientific terms for things that when put together form the mystical concept of "cozy."* It is apparent that among even the best rational creations of the new architecture there has been a lack of filling precisely such requirements as those listed above, which are the dearest to people and often are components of the requirements for which we have used emotionally tinged words.

In other words, we can say that one of the ways to arrive at a more and more humanely built environment is to expand the concept rational. *We should rationally analyze more of the requirements connected with the object than we have to date.* All the different requirements imaginable that can be made of an object's quality form a sort of scale, perhaps a series similar to a spectrum. In the red field of the spectrum lie social viewpoints, in the orange field questions connected with production, etc., all the way to the invisible ultraviolet field, where perhaps the rationally undefinable requirements, still invisible to us, which exist in the individual human being, are hidden. Whatever the case, it is at the end of the spectrum, where the purely *human* questions reside, where we will make most new discoveries. That these won't be limited to the random examples I mentioned for the metal chair is clear. Even if, as suggested above, we can find on closer analysis that an emotional concept is among other things a sum of physically measurable quantities, we still will quickly find ourselves outside the realm of physics. *A series of requirements that can be made of almost every object and that up to now has been given scant consideration surely belongs in the sphere of another science—psychology. As soon as we include psychological requirements, or, let us say, when we can do so, then we will have already expanded the rational method to an extent that, to a greater degree than previously, has the potential of excluding inhuman results.*

I permit myself to go from the tubular steel chair to another example, the lighting fixture. Tradition in this branch is candlelight, and why not oil lamps as well? The equipment, all the way from chandeliers to oil lamp shades, has gallantly followed us into the era of electricity. This is not tradition—it is *kitsch.*

As far as lighting is concerned, modernism has mostly had shiny white porcelain balls and opal cubes to show, and even serious rational producers have pursued approximately the same line. Without doubt a closed, dust free porcelain ball with nickel hanger is acceptable from a manufacturing viewpoint. It is usually a little worse in terms of lighting economy. But one item that is most often ignored or in any case neglected is the quality of the light. What do we mean by the light's quality? Light exists for man, a phenomenon he needs without interruption at his disposal. Properly adapted quality is in other words much more important in this case than in the case of objects whose contact with humans is merely temporary. We meet here the same phenomenon as everywhere else: an acceptable perfection from a purely technical viewpoint—

fixtures, their movable parts, their methods of manufacture, etc., have received their rational treatment but from many different viewpoints, their main task, lighting as man's good servant, its adaptability for good vision, and in general its quality in relationship to man, has fallen behind. In this field, if anywhere, people have tried to improve upon this lack with inappropriate glued-on forms. English parchment shades with Piranesi pictures and similar things have had to represent "hominess."

Equally, modernism has created an enormous number of piquant chandeliers, porcelain tube-mounted lights, soffit lighting, etc. The failure to deal rationally with vision requirements and man's psychological needs is perhaps not a sin immediately recognized in an ordinary home. But if we go from the private home to, let us say, a hospital, where we have to deal with masses of people in a weakened condition, we soon notice that we cannot correct any failings with the "cozy" remedies I have mentioned. In a person weakened by sickness there are psychic irritations and physical sensitivities that lie close to the psychic (irritation of the optic nerves among them) in an exaggerated manner. I have myself had experience of this in my practice. It was apparent that the prevalent hospital lighting, opalescent white bodies of light, was highly unsuitable and above all psychically irritating, even in cases where the light fixtures' glare level was reduced to a minimum. The fixtures' prevalent placement, the classical middle-of-the-ceiling principle, had to be revised, and general lighting for the room arranged solely with consideration for the sick person, his horizontal position, etc. Each solution is in some way a compromise that is most easily discovered when one considers man in his weakest condition.

A very notable pitfall in the possibility of creating a humane fixture, a humane light, should be noted: there exist very few possibilities of examining the light's quality so thoroughly as in spectrolanalysis. There is even less possibility, naturally, of creating a light with a spectrum properly adapted to humans. The difficulties are increased by the fact that there is such a large quantitative difference between sunlight and artificial light. It has been suggested that we cannot achieve good results by giving artificial light the same spectrum as sunlight because man is dependent on the large quantities of certain parts of the spectrum in sunlight. In accordance with this it has even been said that the candle's yellow flame and the interior decorator lady's inclination to glorify her light compositions with yellow silk rags come closer to the mark vis-à-vis human instincts than the electrical technician with his luxmeter and his schematic concept of "white light."

We can in other words accept the criticism that much of rational lighting is inhumane. But the example from the hospital has already shown that an improvement will not be achieved by the design of formalistic lighting fixtures, whether they are traditional or modern. We can perhaps arrive at piquant effects via formal solutions, lamps that look amusing when turned off, etc., but we cannot build a lighting "culture" in the era of electricity through this type of dilettantism. Instead we should expand the rational approach so that it includes more requirements connected to the problem. We should rationally examine the technical and the general hygienic needs all the way to that borderline where the psychological needs begin and even over this line to the best of our abilities. That the experience of the long and rich tradition of the applied arts can here give us valuable study material is of course clear. I mean the genuine tradition and its historical development, but not the traditionalism that survives formally and inorganically. I am inclined to say that history gives us a kind of statistic on how man reacts to his environment, and in this respect, as has been suggested above, candlelight could also become an important study material in a technohumane laboratory, which would solve the question of what is the most rational artificial light for man.

I have dealt here with two groups of examples, the chair on which man sits and the light in which, so to speak, he swims about. I have tried to show that the rational work done during the manufacture and design of the objects has by no means led to its definite goal; that mistakes and weaknesses—they must be legion—are not of the type that dilettantism and grafting on of inorganic and questionable

formal elements can help overcome. I have meant to say that the correct meaning of rationalism is to process all the questions that concern the object, to deal rationally also with the requirements that are often regarded as undefinable individual questions of taste but that on closer analysis show themselves to be partly neurological, partly psychological questions, etc. Salvation can come only or primarily through an expanded rationality. That this is also the case in a large number of other areas within the design industry one finds quite often. Color problems, which to a certain extent belong to the same category as lighting and where psychological research, naturally, should have something to offer, are in general also neglected. In regard to this, as in so many other areas, there is a particular factor from the psychic world that rational architecture has dealt with relatively well. I mean the question of variability, the possibility of interaction between man and his environment and his objects, where the environment fulfills the psychological need for constant regeneration and change. An ordinary cure for present-day man's nervous disorders is changing his environment. It is obvious that his most intimate surroundings should be created with what I would almost like to call the automatic possibility of constant change. It is clear that a great many sins have been committed, especially as concerns colors, textiles, etc. As we meet here a psychological requirement that the new architecture truly has been intuitively concerned with, we should admit that this is one of the main reasons why the gluing on of traditional and modern decoration is unsuitable. Decoration, monumentality, forced adaptability of forms are all things that subtract from an object's possibilities of variation. As long as standardization is the production principle it should be regarded as highly inhumane to produce formalism. A standard article should not be a definitive product; it should on the contrary be made so that the form is completed by man himself according to all the individual laws that involve him. Only in the case of objects that have a neutral quality can standardization's coercion of the individual be softened and its positive side culturally exploited. There is a civilization that, even in its traditional phase, its handicraft era, showed enormous sensitivity and tact toward the individual in this regard. I mean parts of the Japanese culture, which, with its limited range of raw materials and forms, inculcated a virtuoso skill in creating variations and almost daily recombinations. Its great predilection for flowers, plants, and natural objects is a unique example. The contact with nature and its constantly observable change is a way of life that has difficulty getting along with concepts that are too formalistic.

But even the psychological element in the new applied arts, within its rational working domain, if I may express it so, still exists in the Bronze Age. It is the purely social education of large masses of people that is lacking here; therefore formalism sold by advertising techniques still has a good market. People get objects with standardized forms and ready-made standardized decorations, which, because of these same characteristics, hinder them from creating an environment for themselves with a living, natural, constantly changing character.

We have thus come back to the question of form as such. A constantly changing environment means that there is after all a form that should be independent of how things are constructed. We have already touched upon the importance of variability. Nature, biology, is formally rich and luxuriant. It can with the same structure, the same intermeshing, and the same principles in its cells' inner structure, achieve a billion combinations, each of which represents a high level of form. Man's life belongs to the same family. The things surrounding him are hardly fetishes and allegories with a mystical eternal value. They are rather cells and tissues, living beings also, building elements of which human life is put together. They cannot be treated differently from biology's other elements or otherwise they run the risk of not fitting into the system; they become inhuman.

Lecture given at the annual meeting of the Swedish Craft Society, May 9, 1935

51

25. Landscape near Bern, 1947

52

26. Eruption of the volcano Heklas. From an airplane trip, 1947

Island Hekla

47

54

28. Landscape. From a trip to Italy, 1948

56

30. Landscape, Epila, 1951

EPILA
Somma-51

31. Landscape, Salillas de Jalón, 1951

58

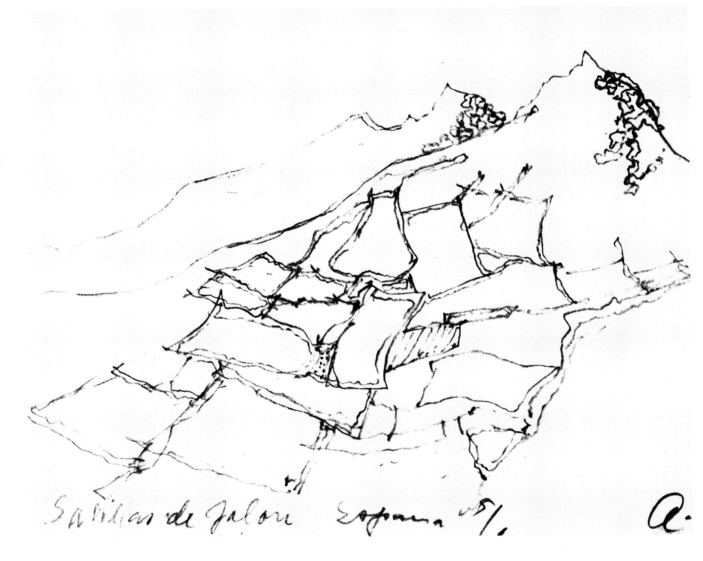

Salillas de Jalon   Espana 51

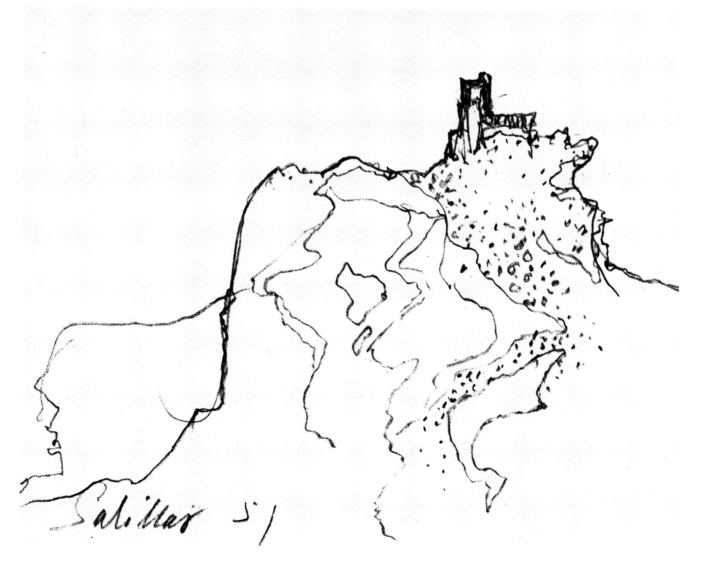

The Influence of Construction and Materials on Modern Architecture

Building materials and construction methods do not by themselves exert a onesided and direct influence on architecture.

In ancient times (Mykonos) or in even earlier ages, when the possibilities of processing materials were nonexistent or slight, it was nature itself in its capacity as the only provider of materials that restricted all possibilities of building in a deviant manner. One could perhaps call the art of architecture during these primitive times an "art of discovery." Because of the lack of possibilities for processing, it was imperative to find ready-made building materials in nature. Blocks of stone, tree trunks, and animal skins were perhaps the likeliest choices, and the art of architecture was a matter of combining them correctly.

This primitive art arouses in us remarkable feelings of admiration, for of course it most clearly demonstrates to us the human intellect's first modest triumphs over raw and untouched nature. In this connection one can undoubtedly speak of the absolute and direct effect of materials and methods on architecture. Indeed, one may also call it a relentless dependence.

But as architecture evolves it becomes less simple to correlate cause and effect. Instead of "materials direct from nature," we get building materials; they are no longer a group of original and undeveloped materials but are subject to constantly changing methods of treatment, treatment that continues during the process of construction itself.

The art of architecture has, in a sense, created its world of materials and methods itself. In a deeper sense, architecture is not merely finished buildings, but rather a variegated process of development that, thanks to an internal reciprocal action, constantly leads to new solutions, new forms, new building materials, and constant changes in the ideology of construction.

But if, instead of talking about the influence of materials and construction methods on architecture, we modestly attempt to examine this inner process and try to follow its curve, we should have a better chance at achieving an understanding of it. The shape of this curve of development for the past, present, and future makes it possible for us to reach important conclusions concerning building even in our own time.

In primitive times the bearing structure was essentially the only problem as well as being the basic element of architecture. Walls, openings, and the post and lintel system essentially made up "the art of architecture." Relatively late, during the Hellenic period, most details and detail groupings were still essentially small protuberances on the structural frame itself and often practically inseparable from it. From Mykonos to the Parthenon, we see lintels of natural stone treated in the same manner as the stones in the thick walls. Most problems of detailing were solved as soon as the bearing frame of the building was completed.

Today, on the other hand, the structure, ancient architecture's only basic element, is reduced to a light metal frame, and producing this frame is but an unimportant part of the total construction process. Perhaps this iron frame calls to mind the tent construction of primitive times, yet it differs from it in one important respect—the frame of a modern building is often in its volume, and certainly in its importance, always a smaller part of the total building than its counterpart in ancient times. And as the frame's importance has diminished, other problems and basic new elements have arisen in the building process.

In man's struggle with nature one can trace through the ages a conscious striving to treat each problem so that its importance and its threat to human existence is effectively reduced. If we analyze architecture from this point of view, as a component in the struggle between man and nature, we find its essential character to be a systematic, continual changeability. In the internal processes, the problems and thus also the number of basic architectural elements are continually increasing, but at the same time questions that have been of prime concern lose their importance. This natural thematic fluctuation is one of architecture's most basic characteristics, and it is essential that we allow for it in our own work today.

Within the profession of architecture there is (not least of all in our time) a formal conservatism that strives to give architectural programs of the most varied character an identical form. This misunderstanding of the stylistic term Gleichgestaltung is, especially when it occurs on a large scale, one of the main obstacles to the realization of architecture's inner essence. In order to achieve its task, which is to aid in the solution of wide-ranging humanistic, socioeconomic, and psychological problems, architecture must be allowed as much internal and formal flexibility as possible.

Every formal straitjacket, whether it be a deep-rooted stylistic tradition or a superficial uniformity born out of a misunderstanding of modern architecture, prevents architecture from playing its full part in the human struggle for existence; in other words, lessens its significance and effectiveness.

There are obviously many reasons that schematic forms have a stunting effect on a more vital architecture. One of them especially should be mentioned—town planning and all the regulations connected with it. In modern town planning practice we encounter all too many circumstances that determine and limit in advance the character of a prospective building. Town planning practice has become a kind of building inspector that has pushed itself too far into the reality of architecture and thereby become an obstacle to its natural and fundamental development, and thus also to its ability to fulfill its task.

Already the fact that the first basic element of architecture—the structure—has changed character in the manner described above means that we today, when faced with a building task, have to choose between an infinitely greater number of solutions than before. At the same time it means that it is more difficult to define in advance the building's characteristics. Town planning regulations and legislation that, for instance, attempt to prevent land from being exploited in a socially disadvantageous manner, and thereby regulate the height, ground area, and siting of prospective buildings, often, even their very form, are exceeding their essential task. Instead of acting in a stimulating manner on development they have become an obstacle to it.

Earlier I discussed an architectural element whose developmental stages can be traced all the way back to its primitive beginning. We will see that even other elements that became a part of architecture at a later date have gone through similar stages of development. Let us, for example, examine more closely the problems of insulation; the whole range of problems that begin with insulation against the forces of nature and end with insulation between people and groups of people.

Insulation was originally a question of planning (for lack of other means, most insulation problems were solved through a choice of building sites), but subsequent developments have given us innumerable materials and methods for technical solutions to this type of problem. Water pressure insulation has given us the opportunity to penetrate deeper into the earth. Different combinations of insulation materials have, on occasion, changed the nature of roof construction and finally led to, among other things, the independence of the flat roof from all considerations of global latitude. This latter phenomenon has led to the freeing of the floor plan from the dominance exercised previously by the roof structure. From an important consideration, the roof structure has been reduced to a flexible and less important factor, and we now have innumerable new possibilities for previously unknown floor plan solutions. Equally, different materials, by increasing the effectiveness of acoustical insulation, have made it possible for us to place people in greater proximity to each other without the problems this previously led to.

All this is new proof of the structural changes taking place in architecture.

If we further examined some other groups of elements, for example, the movable parts of a building, or if we examined the whole range of surface treatments from those subject to heavy wear, to those used to amplify or damp sound, we would come to a conclusion that points in the same direction. To the extent that the number of industrially produced building materials, of standard parts, and of methods increases, the number of possible combinations also increases and with it the flexibility in all building design.

Technical services form a separate group within modern building. The problems they solve are essentially old ones, but one can say that these technical methods free the basic systems from their old contexts and thus increase the internal freedom in building design.

I shall give only one example: the heating system. We are today, without exception, accustomed to central heating. The feasibility studies for such a plant indicate that it cannot be achieved in the most economical manner for merely a medium-sized building. Here, as in other purely technical questions, there appears the clear desirability of certain efforts toward centralization. I myself have just completed an installation where many different buildings were joined up to one central heating plant by means of an underground piping system, a solution that has already been used many times in various parts of the world.

What this will mean to town planning, for example, is quite clear; the boundaries of a lot or whole blocks cannot be determined arbitrarily in advance. They, and to an even greater degree the relationship of buildings to each other, will become dependent on the different buildings' internal heating systems. The fact that we are at the same time achieving the possibility of electric heating, which in its turn frees buildings from any dependence on each other in relation to the heating system, is an additional proof of the structural changes taking place in architecture that I mentioned earlier.

One further phenomenon in architecture should be called to mind in this context, the oldest and at the same time the most recent technique: standardization. Standardization has always existed, is in fact one of the most important factors in helping to create systematization in architecture. Standardization is usually seen as a method that makes everything uniform and schematic. It is clear that this is not so. Properly standardized building elements and raw materials are such that one can achieve a wide variety of results by combining them in different ways. I once suggested that nature herself is the world's best standards committee, but in nature standardization is practiced almost exclusively in the smallest possible units, the cells.

This results in millions of different combinations that never become schematic. Another result is an infinite richness of constantly changing, organically growing forms.

In opposition to the view that sees established forms and uniformity as the only way to achieve architectural harmony and successfully controlled building techniques, I have tried with all I have said here to emphasize that architecture's inner nature is a fluctuation and a development suggestive of natural organic life. I would like to maintain that this is finally the only true style in architecture. If obstacles are placed in this path architecture will wither and die. As we are gathered here today for the Nordic Building Conference, a conference whose purpose is to create the conditions for a better architecture, we have every reason to attempt to eliminate all factors that stand in the way of its achievement. This leads me back to town planning. Representatives of different countries should attempt in their countries to influence development in such a direction that all types of zoning and preliminary planning, based on a view of architecture insensitive to the possibilities for growth and inner variations, be replaced by systems with greater development capability.

Town planning development must be channeled in such a manner that flats, houses, and groups of houses are always designed in a manner natural to the time in which they are conceived. The internal grouping of houses should be freely developed according to programmatic requirements, and all regulations that aim at a superficial formal unity should be rejected. Our communities should, step by step, evolve out of the free grouping of buildings whose internal relationships are both aesthetically satisfying and functionally without points of friction. Instead of monotony, town planning should strive to create the freedom for a true and proper development. It should be a flexible system that makes it possible to control the growth of communities, especially in relation to the physiological, social, and psychological problems they face.

Lecture given at the Nordic Building Conference, Oslo, 1938

World's Fairs:
The New York World's Fair and the Golden Gate Exposition

[In 1939 the American Federation of Arts invited to its annual convention in Washington exhibition architects from France, England, Finland, Sweden, and Brazil to discuss their work and their attitude to current artistic concerns. Following is an excerpt from Alvar Aalto's speech at the convention.]

Unfortunately I lack the means to explain to you solely in words what we have tried to say with the Finnish pavilion and the exhibition. Exhibitions are in and of themselves a kind of "accounting," but they should derive their impact from their substance, not from words. Therefore I would like to mention here only one fact about the Finnish exhibition and the basic principles of its assemblage. We have tried to leave out as much as possible of what we couldn't bring from Finland to New York in demonstrable, concrete, visual form.

Objects by themselves can hardly give a convincing picture of a country; it can only arise out of the atmosphere created by the objects and constitutes, in other words, a totality that can only be grasped instinctively. Because I am conscious of this I cannot explain the design principles behind the Finnish exhibition, much less say whether this exhibition has hit the mark.

With your permission I would instead like to use your time for another purpose. I would like to deal briefly with some common problems, important both for America and for Finland.

The splendid exhibitions in New York and San Francisco that America has just assembled demonstrate in their own manner that such a form of activity is necessary as a universal cultural activity. The world needs, alongside and as a counterweight to the purely literary medium, a means of communication based on material things if our civilization is to be kept in balance. Despite the fact that the large exhibitions no longer play such a pure and constructive role as in an earlier time, I consider that today they are if possible even more important for us. And that today, properly used and planned, they have a purpose that if anything is greater than has ever before been possible. We could make them into a permanent national educational institution in every country so that, taken together, they constituted a kind of universal school, shared by all countries.

Historically, the first era of the great exhibitions coincided with the strongest expansionist period of our current civilization. The exhibitions of the time functioned like large generators and impulse distributors. But especially noteworthy is their important function as experimental institutions for technical and planning problems. Thus I have indirectly said that the exhibitions of today, as a consequence of weak organization, do not have this same broad significance. Their character must be transformed if they are to fulfill their task in a new era. Let us just imagine that the sums of money that have been spent on the exhibitions in New York and San Francisco instead had been used purposefully for an equally comprehensive experimental effort and been concentrated on the most important problems of our time, those represented by housing, the city, and traffic together. If these two exhibitions had been the end of an effort in this direction they would surely have resulted in an advance so large and so clearly recognized that one could express it in terms of a considerable percentage. With what I have just said I have attempted to underline the original vitality of the great exhibitions and to suggest the possibility of giving them back this purpose as motors for humanity's development. I am sure that in this manner they would also achieve a solid economic base, not to speak of the fact that they would inform people (the so-called public) about the valuable experimental activity, over its whole comprehensive range, that begins with primitive inquisitiveness and ends in that drive to creative work which exists in every individual.

The main part consists here, as all over the world, of the intrinsic, practical, and reliable exhibition material that, without any additional narrative propaganda, in other words, without go-betweens, is presented to the public. American machines, tools, treatment processes for food, and examples of their overall organization that the general public usually doesn't see—all these are things of which I have found beautiful and instructive examples.

But alongside all this there exists at both these exhibitions, as at all the great exhibitions I have seen up till now, a great deal of unnecessary decorative material, an irrelevant architectural shell that, as a rule, remains irrelevant. It is absolutely certain, for example, that the thorough

presentation at the New York World's Fair of the machinery on a normal American farm and the whole life and organization that exists on the farm interested the public more than the decorative constructions, one more enormous than the other, where the propaganda is the shell for a content either too insignificant or, to use a "tomorrow" word, too utopian. As I see it, this element of industrial design in the exhibition's composition lacks architectural seriousness. It appears to be un-American and of a transitory nature. During my trips in your country I have seen an America that in no way fits the gaudy colors and unmotivated contours that dominate the exhibition area. On the contrary, I have seen an America where exaggerations are rare or belong in the realm of humor, while life's content instead is a kind of economic philosophy that willingly leaves out everything superfluous to the structure's task or to primary comfort.

We all know what so-called exhibition fatigue means. If we wished to examine the nature of this phenomenon more closely we would find that it essentially depends on the effect of two different toxins. It is partly physical and partly psychological in nature. The physical tiredness can be eliminated through correct site planning of the exhibitions and through certain mechanical aids, less of the latter as they easily increase the psychological exhaustion symptoms. It surprised me, though, that the planning was not on a level with the exhibition's size. In a climate such as New York's I had expected continuous covered arcades to protect against rain and heat, and a traffic system that could have been something along the lines of the New York subway system, with different speeds, different tour systems, and periodic stops at different exhibition areas. The question of psychological fatigue is again tied to the formal language that has been used. An exaggerated decorativeness, both in terms of buildings and exhibition techniques, begins rapidly to tire rather than stimulate us. Also, from this viewpoint the "industrial design" system becomes an un-American element that creates disturbances in the exhibition machinery.

65

"Maailmannäyttelyt: New York World's Fair/The Golden Gate Exposition," *Arkkitehti*, 1939

E. G. Asplund in Memoriam

Sweden—but above all, architecture—has suffered a great loss. The foremost among architects, who in a wider sense has been both pioneer and pathfinder for the living architecture of his own era, has left us. Gunnar Asplund's death has deprived Scandinavia of an irreplaceable architect. Though his buildings exist intact, as should be the case with an architect's work, the personal loss is irreparable.

Asplund's contribution to the architectural battles of our age was exclusively that of the architect, not that of the dialectician which is alien to the art of architecture. Like many of those colleagues who shared his goals, he strove to create harmony in his work, to tie together the threads of a living future with those of a living past. In the creation of forms, pastiche and copying were as alien to him as rootless technocratic constructivism.

He avoided imitating architecture's own forms just as he shunned a dry constructivism; instead he found a direct path to nature and its world of forms. I received a vivid impression of this aspect of his work even on first meeting Asplund. We sat in Scandia's indigo colored theater a few days before it was completed. "While I was building this I thought of autumn evenings and yellow leaves," said Asplund as he showed me the contourless auditorium with its yellow light fixtures. I had the impression that this was an architecture where ordinary systems hadn't served as the parameters. Here the point of departure was man, with all the innumerable nuances of his emotional life and nature. This contact with nature, man included, was clearly discernible in all of Asplund's projects. Much can be written about Asplund's art and its different phases, but if one studies them one will always find this underlying direct contact with nature.

The motifs of a large proportion of our conventional architecture still are fragments of a bygone era. Another architecture has arrived, which builds for man and essentially regards people as a social phenomenon, while at the same time taking science and research as the point of departure. But beyond that a newer architecture has made its appearance, one that continues to employ the tools of the social sciences, but that also includes the study of psychological problems—"the unknown human" in his totality. The latter has proved that the art of architecture continues to have inexhaustible resources and means which flow directly from nature and the inexplicable reactions of human emotions. Within this latter architecture, Asplund has his place.

"E. G. Asplund in Memoriam," *Arkkitehti*, 1940

Calatanao Sopano 57,

38. Three windmills. From a trip to Spain, 1951

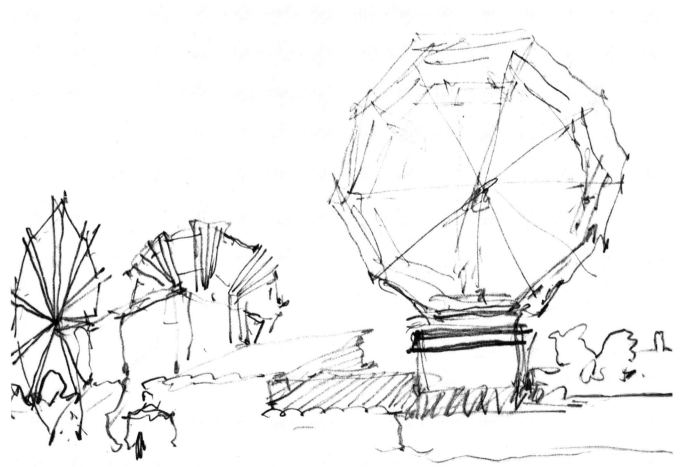

39. Landscape with windmill. From a trip to Spain, 1951

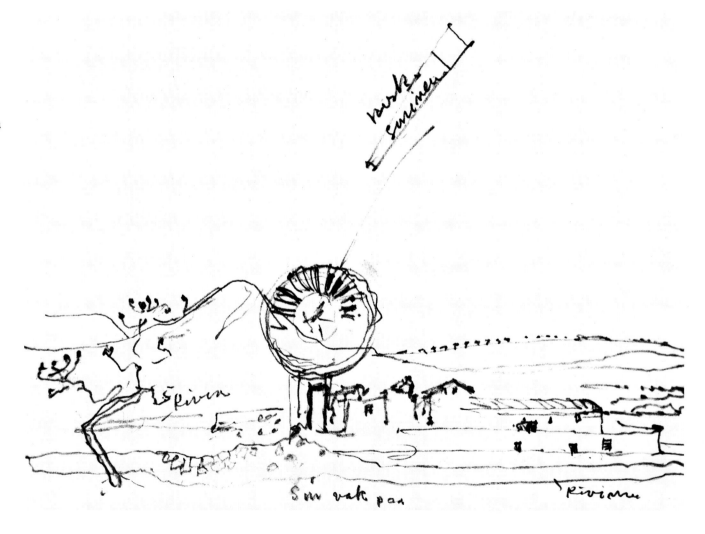

40. Farm. From a trip to Spain, 1951

The Humanizing of Architecture

In contrast with that architecture whose main concern is the formalistic style a building shall wear, stands the architecture that we know as functionalism. The development of the functional idea and its expression in structures are probably the most invigorating occurrences in architectural activity in our time, and yet function in architecture—and so also functionalism—are not so very easy to interpret precisely. "Function" is the characteristic use, or work, or action of a thing. "Function" is also a thing or quantity that depends upon, and varies with, another. "Functionalism" the dictionaries boldly define as "conscious adaptation of form to use"—it is both less and more than that, for truly it must recognize and reckon with both of the meanings of "function."

Architecture is a synthetic phenomenon covering practically all fields of human activity. An object in the architectural field may be functional from one point of view and unfunctional from another. During the past decade, modern architecture has been functional chiefly from the technical point of view, with its emphasis mainly on the economic side of the building activity. Such emphasis is desirable, of course, for production of good shelters for the human being has been a very expensive process as compared with the fulfillment of some other human needs. Indeed, if architecture is to have a larger human value, the first step is to organize its economic side. But, since architecture covers the entire field of human life, real functional architecture must be functional mainly from the human point of view. If we look deeper into the processes of human life, we shall discover that technique is only an aid, not a definite and independent phenomenon therein. Technical functionalism cannot create definite architecture.

If there were a way to develop architecture step by step, beginning with the economic and technical aspect and later covering the other more complicated human functions, then the purely technical functionalism would be acceptable; but no such possibility exists. Architecture not only covers all fields of human activity; it must even be developed in all these fields at the same time. If not, we shall have only one-sided, superficial results.

The term "rationalism" appears in connection with modern architecture about as often as does "functionalism." Modern architecture has been rationalized mainly from the technical point of view, in the same way as the technical functions have been emphasized. Although the purely rational period of modern architecture has created constructions where rationalized technique has been exaggerated and the human functions have not been emphasized enough, this is not a reason to fight rationalization in architecture. It is not the rationalization itself that was wrong in the first and now past period of modern architecture. The wrongness lies in the fact that the rationalization has not gone deep enough. Instead of fighting rational mentality, the newest phase of modern architecture tries to project rational methods from the technical field out to human and psychological fields.

It might be well to have an example: One of the typical activities in modern architecture has been the construction of chairs and the adoption of new materials and new methods for them. The tubular steel chair is surely rational from technical and constructive points of view: It is light, suitable for mass production, and so on. But steel and chromium surfaces are not satisfactory from the human point of view. Steel is too good a conductor of heat. The chromium surface gives too bright reflections of light, and even acoustically is not suitable for a room. The rational methods of creating this furniture style have been on the right track, but the result will be good only if rationalization is exercised in the selection of materials which are most suitable for human use.

The present phase of modern architecture is doubtless a new one, with the special aim of solving problems in the humanitarian and psychological fields. This new period, however, is not in contradiction to the first period of technical rationalization. Rather, it is to be understood as an enlargement of rational methods to encompass related fields.

During the past decades architecture has often been compared with science, and there have been efforts to make its methods more scientific, even efforts to make it a pure science. But architecture is not a science. It is still the same great synthetic process of combining thousands of definite human functions, and remains *architecture*. Its purpose is still to bring the material world into harmony with human life. To make architecture more human means better architecture, and it means a functionalism much larger than the merely technical one. This goal can be accomplished only by architectural methods—by the creation and combination of different technical things in such a way that they will provide for the human being the most harmonious life.

Architectural methods sometimes resemble scientific ones, and a process of research, such as science employs, can be adopted also in architecture. Architectural research can be more and more methodical, but the substance of it can never be solely analytical. Always there will be more of instinct and art in architectural research.

Scientists very often use exaggerated forms in analyses in order to obtain clearer, more visible results—bacteria are stained, and so on. The same methods can be adopted in architecture, also. I have had personal experience with hospital buildings where I was able to discover that especial physical and psychological reactions by patients provided good pointers for ordinary housing. If we proceed from technical functionalism, we shall discover that a great many things in our present architecture are unfunctional from the point of view of psychology or a combination of psychology and physiology. To examine how human beings react to forms and construction, it is useful to use for experimentation especially sensitive persons, such as patients in a sanatorium.

Experiments of this kind were performed in connection with the Paimio Tuberculosis Sanatorium building in Finland and were carried on mainly in two special fields: (1) the relation between the single human being and his living room; (2) the protection of the single human being against large groups of people and the pressure from collectivity. Study of the relation between the individual and his quarters involved the use of experimental rooms and covered the questions of room form, colors, natural and artificial light, heating system, noise, and so on. This first experiment dealt with a person in the weakest possible condition, a bed patient. One of the special results discovered was the necessity for changing the colors in the room. In many other ways, the experiment showed, the room must be different from the ordinary room. This difference can be explained thus: The ordinary room is a room for a vertical person; a patient's room is a room for a horizontal human being, and colors, lighting, heating, and so on must be designed with that in mind.

Practically, this fact means that the ceiling should be darker, with an especially selected color suitable to be the only view of the reclining patient for weeks and weeks. The artificial light cannot come from an ordinary ceiling fixture, but the principal center of light should be beyond the angle of vision of the patient. For the heating system in the experimental room, ceiling radiators were used but in a way which threw the heat mainly at the foot of the bed so that the head of the patient was outside the direct heat rays. The location of the windows and doors likewise took into account the patient's position. To avoid noise, one wall in the room was sound absorbing, and wash basins (each patient in the two-patient rooms had his own) were especially designed so that the flow of water from the faucet hit the porcelain basin always at a very small angle and worked noiselessly.

These are only a few illustrations from an experimental room at the sanatorium, and they are here mentioned merely as examples of architectural methods, which always are a combination of technical, physical, and psychological phenomena, never any one of them alone. Technical functionalism is correct only if enlarged to cover even the psychophysical field. That is the only way to humanize architecture.

Flexible wooden furniture is a result of experiments also made at the Paimio Sanatorium. At the time of those experiments the first tubular chromium furniture was just being constructed in Europe. Tubular and chromium surfaces are good solutions technically, but psychophysically these materials are not good for the human being. The

sanatorium needed furniture that should be light, flexible, easy to clean, and so on. After extensive experimentation in wood, the flexible system was discovered and a method and material combined to produce furniture that was better for the human touch and more suitable as the general material for the long and painful life in a sanatorium.

The main problem connected with a library is that of the human eye. A library can be well constructed and can be functional in a technical way even without the solving of this problem, but it is not humanly and architecturally complete unless it deals satisfactorily with the main human function in the building, that of reading a book. The eye is only a tiny part of the human body, but it is the most sensitive and perhaps the most important part. To provide a natural or an artificial light that destroys the human eye or that is unsuitable for its use, means reactionary architecture even if the building should otherwise be of high constructive value.

Daylight through ordinary windows, even if they are very large, covers only a part of a big room. Even if the room is lighted sufficiently, the light will be uneven and will vary on different points of the floor. That is why skylights have mainly been used in libraries, museums, and so on. But skylight, which covers the entire floor area, gives an exaggerated light, if extensive additional arrangements are not made. In the library building the problem was solved with the aid of numerous round skylights so constructed that the light could be termed indirect daylight. The round skylights are technically rational because of the monopiece glass system employed. (Every skylight consists of a conical concrete basement six feet in diameter, and a thick jointless round piece of glass on top of it without any frame construction.) This system is humanly rational because it provides a kind of light suitable for reading, blended and softened by being reflected from the conical surfaces of the skylights. In Finland the largest angle of sunlight is almost 52 degrees. The concrete cones are so constructed that the sunlight always remains indirect. The surfaces of the cones spread the light in millions of directions. Theoretically, for instance, the light reaches an open book from all these different directions and thus avoids a reflection to the human eye from the white page of the book. (Bright reflection from book pages is one of the most fatiguing phenomena in reading.) In the same way this lighting system eliminates shadow phenomena regardless of the position of the reader. The problem of reading a book is more than a problem of the eye; a good reading light permits the use of many positions of the human body and every suitable relation between book and eye. Reading a book involves both culturally and physically a strange kind of concentration; the duty of architecture is to eliminate all disturbing elements.

It is possible in a scientific way to ascertain what kinds and what quantities of light are ideally the most suitable for the human eye, but in constructing a room the solution must be made with the aid of all the different elements that architecture embraces. Here the skylight system is a combined product of the ceiling construction (a room almost sixty feet wide needs a ceiling construction with beams high enough for the erection of the deep cones) and special technical limits in horizontal glass construction. An architectural solution must always have a human motive based on analysis, but that motive has to be materialized in construction that probably is a result of extraneous circumstances. The examples mentioned here are very tiny problems. But they are very close to the human being and hence become more important than problems of much larger scope.

"The Humanizing of Architecture," *Technology Review*, 1940

Architecture in Karelia

[Editor's note: This article was written in 1941 while eastern Karelia was occupied by Finnish troops. Alvar Aalto later saw a formal connection between the multistory gabled houses in Karelia and the *bojar* farmhouses in the Novgorod area. Despite this architecture-historical error, the text deserves attention because it shows Aalto's strong feeling for organic solutions within vernacular architecture and illustrates his vision of a purely functional architecture independent of all styles.]

The old Karelian architecture is contemporary with the *Kalevala* and the rune material collected in Karelia, which constitutes the main trunk of Finnish-language literary culture.

Like the rune collectors, Finnish architects and folklore researchers have spent many expeditions studying Karelian architecture and the material culture connected with it. A series of expeditions beginning in the 1890s assumed great importance, not just for researchers but above all for working artists (Gallen-Kallela, Yrjo Blomstedt, Sparre, Sucksdorf, Ullberg, etc.). It was especially the creative elite's interest that caused Karelian architecture to exercise its influence during the period of remarkably intensive cultural activity around the turn of the century when Helsinki received what are even today its most acclaimed buildings (Eliel Saarinen, Lars Sonck).

Unfortunately neither the cultural activity around the turn of the century nor in general the laws that organically bind tradition and influences from the past to today's creative work are particularly well known. As in general, where creativity in architecture and applied arts is concerned, there seem these days to be, even in this case, not only a large number of inaccuracies in circulation among the so-called public but even more fundamental misconceptions. It is not an altogether easy task to correct these. In addition to research, it requires a special architectural-theoretical popular education program, and for this purpose there is generally in civilized countries a special professional corps of architectural critics and social theoreticians. Since Gustave Strengell's death we have unfortunately not had any such person here in Finland. This lack and Karelian architecture's special relevance have induced the undersigned to write this article, despite the fact that literary means of expression are foreign to a practicing architect, and the material can hardly be exhaustively treated in one article, which could even give rise to new misconceptions.

Just now Karelian architecture is topical to the extent that its significance is not limited to the ethnographic and historic. Here we can find values with a direct, purely practical connection to the present.

A very common misconception in this country is that typical Karelian architecture is of Russian origin.

We often encounter the expression "Novgorod houses" to describe the opposite of the western way of building, which is regarded as prevailing in Finland itself. This conception has its origins in a weakly supported theory but it is not limited to theory; its existence has had a practical effect on the way in which Finland, in other words, the government, has handled building questions within its areas of jurisdiction.

It is very difficult to draw lines for formal and material culture and often it is unnecessary, but the idea that "Karelian architecture" is foreign to today's Finland is not correct. Karelian architecture does not represent "the East" in any special way.

The main areas of Karelian building have, as is known, until very recently been to a large degree isolated from Finland, but at the same time there has existed an almost equally wide zone of isolation between these settlement areas and the bases of Russian culture. It seems perhaps paradoxical if we assert that, for example, most cities in Finland have been exposed to a stronger Russian influence than the old Karelian building culture beyond the vast forests. Such an assertion can, however, have good grounds. The town plans for most of our cities bear the mark of planning influenced by the Empire style of the Russian czars and are in many respects quite similar to the plans of the Empire's provincial cities and government capitals. Also, the results of Engels's era in planning have come to us via St. Petersburg. Of course they bear the mark of the European Enlightenment, which at the time was the dominant trend in the Empire, especially St. Petersburg, but nonetheless they have their source in the native Russian Empire style.

On the other hand, eastern Karelia, which lies within its own vast boundaries, constitutes an architectural reserve, unusual for Europe, where exterior influences have played an unusually small part. By this I mean that the area has to a large extent been obliged to turn to its own resources and has, so to speak, grown organically out of prevailing conditions. Special features, forms, and methods develop out of man's needs, and here one meets the special features of the natural surroundings in remarkably pure form. Karelian architecture has thus an unusual value in that it makes it possible for us to analyze human life's relationship to nature and shows how human life and nature harmonize in the best way in buildings in this geographical area.

In relationship to earlier Finnish architecture, Karelian architecture is perhaps comparable to the *Kalevala* and the history of its origin. Within the isolated east Karelian zone a great deal of architecture has been preserved that has disappeared from present-day Finland but once upon a time existed here.

In Finland one often encounters the belief that the frame as well as the building methods and the life style of Karelian buildings are foreign to western Finland and in some way un-Finnish, while the decoration and surface treatment that are part of this building style are understood as mirroring the happy Karelian nature and thus as the very source of Finnish decorative art. One can say, however, that the situation is almost the exact opposite. Decoration and ornamental elements have a very superficial relationship with the architecture's basic characteristics. They are by nature lighter and more superficial phenomena and therefore more sensitive to outside influences. Thus there exist in Karelian architecture, and especially in its decorative elements, certain features that have a clear connection with the culture, Byzantine in origin, which we could call Russian. The building itself, including the plan, has, on the other hand, always remained an expression in a deeper architectural sense, of the prevalent conditions and the people's character. And in this deeper meaning we also find the values that are worth studying. The real results of such a study can be of significance to our life today.

The first essential feature of interest is Karelian architecture's uniformity. There are few comparable examples in Europe. It is a pure forest-settlement architecture in which wood dominates almost one hundred percent both as material and as jointing method. From the roof, with its massive system of joists, to the movable building parts wood dominates, in most cases naked, without the dematerializing effect that a layer of paint gives. In addition, wood is often used in as natural proportions as possible, on the scale typical of the material. A dilapidated Karelian village is somehow similar in appearance to a Greek ruin, where, also, the material's uniformity is a dominant feature, though marble replaces wood. By making this comparison I am not in any way trying to fan some kind of Finnish chauvinism; it is a purely instinctive association whose justification experts surely could recognize.

Another significant special feature is the manner in which the Karelian house has come about, both its historical development and its building methods. Without going further into ethnographic details, we can conclude that the inner system of construction results from a methodical accommodation to circumstance. The Karelian house is in a way a building that begins with a single modest cell or with an imperfect embryo building, shelter for man and animals and which then figuratively speaking grows year by year. "The expanded Karelian house" can in a way be compared with a boilogical cell formation. The possibility of a larger and more complete building is always open.

This remarkable ability to grow and adapt is best reflected in the Karelian building's main architectural principle, the fact that the roof angle isn't constant.

Just this fact, the apparently arbitrary handling of the roof angle, makes possible this conglomerate building that suggests a crystal-type cluster. In and of itself, this free-roof-angle principle is a rather unusual, not to say very rare, phenomenon. In conventional architecture, which

often develops from foreign literary influences or, for example, from the propaganda of imperialistic influences, the roof angle is frozen into position without exception and in the end is most often a typical artificial unifying factor. In the refined, free-roof formations of Karelian architecture, which nonetheless do not lack a system, we find, in other words, a refreshing closeness to nature, a kind of fight for existence that has succeeded in creating exactly the organically living and flexible forms necessary both for the fight and for existence.

This singular architectural freedom is of interest especially for our time. Certainly our era's architectural work of renewal, the renaissance we see the world over, has purposefully striven to free architectural forms and to reach toward a flexible building and town planning totality. And in so doing it has come to almost exactly the same solution as this building culture of what are, from a European point of view, distant forest settlements. Even for the latest architectural renaissance, the first demand is that the prevalent stereotyped roof construction must be made more flexible, vary from flat roofs to sloping ones of different angles. Even if the photographic material is weak, it still gives us a certain idea of how beautifully the roof angles in the Karelian village, in their variations from flat to peaked, adapt themselves to nature, and how the building complex forms a living, constantly changing, and unlimited architectural totality.

In a way the elasticity that characterizes Karelian architecture can even be viewed as a historical precedent for the reconstruction work that is waiting in the now devastated Finland.

The devastation will force us to severe economies but at the same time to rapid building on a scale that has never been eperienced here. This building task is so big that it cannot be carried out with peacetime means. We cannot build ordinary building coplexes; the task will force us to a sensible social building process in which our point of departure is the individual inhabitant, from a small and modest building cell. The task presupposes an architectural system according to which houses can grow and be enlarged over the years. We cannot accomplish our work with the conventional cultural loans or the "technocratic" rationalism and building methods that have been dominant in Europe in recent times. The system must be created here and must take our own circumstances into consideration; but certain features in the Karelian building system that I have just mentioned can give us some excellent help in finding the right system, at least to the extent that larger population groupings, thanks to this architecture, become accessory to the necessary self-confidence and feeling that we are not taking the wrong path.

In a way, the uniformity of materials I spoke of also gives this architecture contact with our time. The lack of building materials caused by the war, which apparently will continue for a good part of the reconstruction period we have before us forces us more than ever before to use our own resources, just as Karelian architecture, as a result of its isolation, has been forced to do through the ages.

I mentioned the less solid connection of the surface decoration with the structure itself. In a way, this decorative element, which, as I mentioned, has strangely enough been affected by foreign influences to a greater extent than the architecture, has often interested the public, even the researchers, more than the architecture itself. In the area of architectural and ethnographic research on the individual Karelian house and house clusters, much remains to be done.

In this architecture there is, in addition to the decoration and ornament, another art form, more organic in its origin. It is mainly based on construction, jointing methods, and, for example, furniture joints. In this sense it is a distinctive art close to nature.

The art form of Karelian furniture is based, like the buildings proper, on the growing tree. While the tree's standard part, the trunk, is used for the buildings, the smaller but formally richer parts of the material, the naturally shaped branches and often even peculiar formations, are used for the furniture.

One would have to search to find an affinity to nature more logical in its beauty—the tall fir tree represents the

building, its knotty branches and sculptural parts the furniture and movable parts.

And in this respect the Karelian building culture has an intimate contact with the present. I know from personal experience the time about ten years ago when "the fight against metal" in interior design was begun, though this business, as far as it concerned me, did not have its source in any sentimental Karelianism.

The Karelian furniture maker's art, which, because of the lack of technical aids, used parts ready-made by nature, achieved at its best a truly brilliant richness of forms and a surprising virtuosity in putting together nature's own shapes into an elegant and practical totality.

A few words about the layout of Karelian village settlements remain to be said.

In this connection one almost always encounters the misapprehension that the Karelian village was chaotically fragmented, labyrinthian in its layout. A critical study shows, however, that the situation is exactly the opposite. Also, the affinity to nature and functional accommodation that doesn't worship the straight line, plays a decisive role here.

When the Karelian village is at its best it uses the terrain's topography, views, and other values in an instructive manner, but precisely because of the villages' isolation the methods of grouping are spontaneous and less subject to formal cultural borrowings than, for example, the western Finnish village settlements, not to speak of the cities. Here we truly have a building *plan*, in the best meaning of the word, that adapts itself to Finnish nature.

"Karjalan rakennustaide," *Uusi Suomi,* 1941

84

42. Fig tree, Spain, 1951

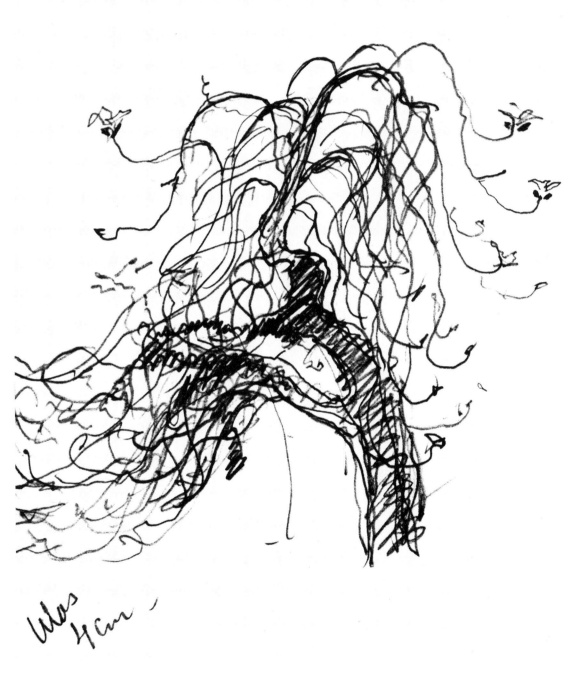

86

46. View westward from Marrakesh, 1951

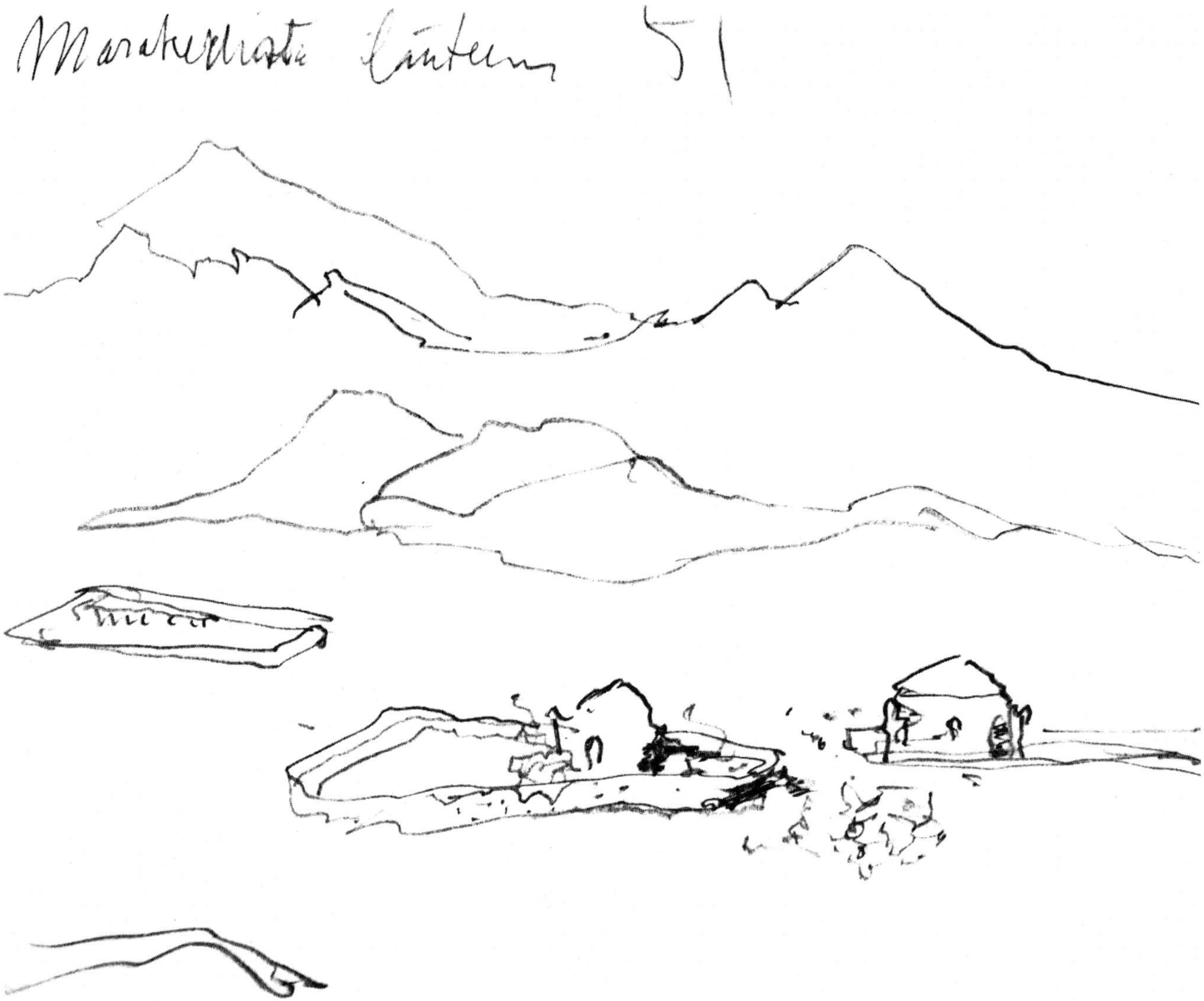

90

48. Above: City wall, Marrakesh, 1951
Below: Houses in Marrakesh, December 9, 1951

91

Building Heights as a Social Problem

The question of a limitation on the height to which one can build, for example, highrise apartment houses, is one of today's most difficult questions. We can say with good reason that the solution has always been a kind of measure of the social level, difficult to define, of different cultural and social organizations. Fundamentally the question is not economic; rather, it is social and psychological factors—often in direct conflict with economic demands—that determine the parameters for housing.

In our neighboring country, Sweden, there has for quite some time been a clear tendency to limit the construction of highrise buildings where they are not regarded as appropriate. One can even say that the Swedish building authorities have seldom allowed buildings of over three stories to be built in provincial towns and other smaller, densely populated areas. The purpose has been partly to preserve the community's own scale and partly to protect an "idyllic" tradition. Similar tendencies have appeared even in our country and many others where the authorities and the society are at all concerned about architecture.

The question of how densely housing should be built is very complex and can hardly be solved only by merely taking into consideration the community's size, population, a possible rural character, or even the desire to preserve an old, idyllic environment.

The author is one of those who only against his will accepts highrise buildings in a location where lowrise building is at all possible. Families with small children should certainly prefer to live in low, scattered housing where all units are at ground level and have direct contact with nature. A home on one level—the original type of human dwelling unit—is clearly superior to other types. Even a two-story house can be regardd as a compromise between the humane and the economic, despite certain practical advantages. Experience has shown, however, that the problems of building in a community cannot be solved in a satisfactory manner merely through the use of the aforementioned ideal form. The social necessity, the technical possibilities, and the economic possibilities—this whole motley bouquet of questions with many unknown factors—leads to a type of residential planning that requires having housing of many different types and combining them with each other. Any decision about which kind of building can be regarded as most appropriate in any given case should, however, be supported by acceptable guidelines of some sort.

As a norm one may clearly hold to the desirability of as high a percentage as possible of single-family dwellings in immediate contact with nature. Under favorable circumstances a well-planned community can realize to a very high percentage such a family-insulated, low-density settlement. But on the other hand every society is composed of different individuals and families, of which some are perhaps quite satisfied with apartments in highrise buildings.

Here, perhaps, someone will say, The higher the worse; but three stories, for example, would appear to be a fairly acceptable limit—keeping in mind present technical possibilities—though it has been found on the other hand that the three-story limit often leads to certain stereotypical solutions. A summary height limitation such as this is not always justified. There are cases in which it is possible to achieve a more advantageous architectural form and greater social and psychological advantages by building real highrise buildings. It is quite posible that a certain number of inhabitants, both families and individuals, belong to that group whose housing problems can be solved in a satisfactory way with highrise apartments, but certainly such a building type cannot satisfy more than 25 percent of the inhabitants. To state my own view, I would say that extra-tall buildings of six or more floors can be defended only where the situation requires such a solution. If the housing site, for example, is by its nature of such a high category that the largest possible number of people should be able to enjoy the advantages it offers, then the construction of highrise buildings may be warranted. If the area in question is located near people's work, if it is convenient to schools and the business center, if it isn't disturbed by factories and heavy traffic, etc., and if it is in addition in every way well located in relationship to the natural sur-

roundings—then the building of highrises may have its logic, even if it deviates from the existing scale of the community.

I would like to point out one circumstance that is often overlooked when weighing questions of this type. Highrise apartments must be regarded, both socially and architecturally, as a considerably more dangerous form of building than single-family houses or lowrise apartments. The highrise building, therefore, presumes a more stringent architectural standard and greater artistry and social responsibility. A badly planned private house or a less successfully planned block of modest lowrise flats disturbs a housing area much less than a badly planned and constructed group of highrise buildings.

In our building legislation and our codes there is not a hint of higher standards in such cases, where a more complicated and responsible task is involved. It must, of course, be admitted that laws can hardly help develop a stronger architectural sense of responsibility. Despite this fact, it is easy to see how building authorities could take advantage of measures of this type. The demands could be for higher technical building standards, greater fire safety, more spacious living quarters (as a compensation for living in a highrise), faultless planning for lighting, views, etc., as well as many other qualitative improvements. And in this connection we should not forget purely aesthetic architectural values and the harmonious placement of buildings in the totality of nature and the surrounding community.

"Rakennuskorkeus sosiaalisesa kysymyksenä," *Arkkitehti,* 1946

93

Culture and Technology

Great ideas arise from the small details of life; they spiral out of the earth. Our senses mediate the raw material, which becomes thoughts. We merely have to make sure that it is we who control the world of the senses, not the other way around.

The freedom that our being demands and industrial mass production have in America arrived at a point of confrontation. At the same time that the American eats well-packaged, well-cooked food and in general enjoys the advantages of systematic mass production, he needs more health care than ever before, because man has not been able really to adjust himself to this new era.

We do not know what is good in man's attitude to his environment and what is bad. We must essentially obey the laws of our own development: and, seen from a sufficient distance, it depends basically on instincts and speculation. America is in any case the country that shows us the whole cultural future of the world, mistakes and all. In America's industrial culture lies not only its whole future development, but its own reflection.

American literature also mirrors this central problem. One could say that man's relationship to industrialism is the most burning problem in modern American literature. American literature is radical. It is striving to show us the reign of terror of industrial mass production over the little man.

Even at the seminar held at Princeton University, the central question was how one could eliminate this reign of terror without losing the blessings industry offers. Participants especially discussed the planning methods for man's physical environment. They reasoned to the minutest detail about the technical aspects of planning of large areas, and then the question was raised, To what extent can overall planning, which does violence to the individual person, be regarded as appropriate, and how much should be left to chance? Common sense and instincts stand here in opposition to each other. With time, instincts will get their due. The present era in planning is an "infant" industrial stage.

America is the land of mass production on an enormous scale. There one has to pay a price many times higher for a customized item. Standardiation involves industrial violence against individual taste. Large laboratories are, however, working on making mass production both more individual and more artistic. Without art, life becomes mechanized, it "dies." There is also an attempt to develop people's artistic tastes, to smuggle taste into their consciousness.

In New York there is a functioning institution in the field of the arts. It strives to deepen a kind of intellectual attitude so that it becomes widely accepted. There arises a group, chosen from proponents of different tastes, whose members, like a swarm of termites, spread the word among the chosen. Even depth is taken into consideration. They eschew general programs and try instead to influence in a deep and lasting fashion certain individuals who will then spontaneously spread their own ideas.

How, then, should planning and individual initiative based on spontaneous activity be brought in line with each other? There are many in the United States who hve thought about this question. How can one subdue a machine without destroying it, how can one preserve industry without "industrializing" man? J. C. Wicker, among others, has raised that question. Production is not the only source of happiness. Man is also a factor to be considered. It is not in things, but in man's attitude toward life that we find the final standard of measurement.

The confrontation of reason and instinct is even mirrored in American humor magazines. In my opinion one must regard *The New Yorker* as the world's foremost humor magazine. The best pieces are Chaplinesque and show man in the stranglehold of mass production. This magazine laughs both at those who unthinkingly want to go "back to nature" and at those who excessively mechanize their existence, especially their spiritual life. In a land where there are streamlined beds and beds without covers—the covers being replaced by an industrially produced layer of warmth—they have truly come far. A gem from *The New Yorker* is the husband who, freezing, hurries to his wife's bed because his own has "shorted."

Whatever finally may happen with reason and instinct, at least for the time being it is America that leads the development, even Europe's part of it. With time, however, the spirit will show itself more powerful than matter.

"Kulttuuri ja Teknikka," *Suomi-Finland—USA*, 1947

The Trout and
the Mountain Stream

For me, as an active artist, it is, of course, difficult to write about questions of art in the same way as would an outsider, like a critic or an art theoretician. He who is himself a professional doesn't have the art historian's objectivity vis-à-vis his colleagues and contemporary creative art. Therefore, the following is only a series of reflections, essentially about my own work.

The question of the link between architecture and art is always with us. Most often it takes the form of a wish that a work of architecture could include more paintings and sculptures. There are different proposals for an organized collaboration between these "three art forms"; sometimes it has almost had the look of a business convention for priests and doctors.

Often the demand has been for more monumental painting in our public buildings! Oddly enough, demands of this sort seldom come from leading artists. Most often they come from a wider stratum of artists or, in the best of cases, as political initiatives from artists' associations or other similar groups.

I am no opponent of these wishes; far from it. The land I feel myself more strongly drawn to than most other countries is Italy, the classical source of unity for the three artistic branches. The news of the destruction of Mantegna's little chapel at Chiesa degli Eremitani caused me a great deal of personal sorrow. But despite this I believe that the question of unification and its solution lie much deeper. In no case can a pure quantitative combination of the three branches reach the core of the problem.

Dr. Ernesto Roger asked me about "architecture's relationship to abstract art." I believe that by this path one may reach deeper, closer to the core of the relationship.

First and foremost, abstract art has given impulses to architecture in our era—indirectly, of course, but the fact cannot be denied. On the other hand, architecture has provided material for abstract art. Each in turn, these two artistic branches have influenced each other. There we have it, in other words—even in our day the arts have common roots and that of course means a great deal.

When I personally have to solve an architectural problem I am confronted, almost always, with an obstacle that is difficult to surmount, a kind of "courage de trois heures du matin." The cause, I believe, is the complicated and intense pressure of the fact that architectural design operates with innumerable elements that internally stand in opposition to each other. They are social, human, economic, and technical demands that unite to become psychological problems with an effect on both the individual and the group, on group and individual movement and internal frictions. All this becomes a maze that cannot be sorted out in a rational or mechanical manner. The large number of different demands and subproblems form an obstacle that is difficult for the architectural concept to break through. In such cases I work—sometimes totally on instinct—in the following manner. For a moment I forget all the maze of problems. After I have developed a feel for the program and its innumerable demands have been engraved in my subconscious, I begin to draw in a manner rather like that of abstract art. Led only by my instincts I draw, not architectural syntheses, but sometimes even childish compositions, and via this route I eventualy arrive at an abstract basis to the main concept, a kind of universal substance with whose help the numerous quarreling subproblems can be brought into harmony.

When I designed the city library at Viipuri (I had plenty of time at my disposal, five whole years) for long periods of time I pursued the solution with the help of primitive sketches. From some kind of fantastic mountain landscapes with cliffs lit up by suns in different positions I gradually arrived at the concept for the library building. The library's architectural core consists of reading and lending areas at different levels and plateaus, while the center and control area forms the high point above the different levels. The childish sketches have only an indirect connection with the architectural conception, but they tied together the section and the plan with each other and created a kind of unity of horizontal and vertical structures.

I recount these personal experiences without wanting to make a method out of them. But I actually think that many of my colleagues have experiencd something similar in their own struggle with architectural problems. The example also has nothing to do with good or bad qualities in the final results. It is just an example of how my own instinctive belief has led me to the fact that architecture and art have a common source, which in a certain sense is abstract, but which despite this is based on the knowledge and the data that we have stored in our subconscious.

At our exhibition in London in 1933 (architect Aino Aalto's and my exhibition was arranged by *Architectural Review*) we had a few wood constructions. The form of a number of them was directly related to forms we had used in our furniture. Others again were experiments with wood forms and methods of treatment without practical value or relationship to everyday life. An art critic in *The Times* wrote about these manifestations of abstract art. He said that they were "nonobjective art" but the results of an inverted creative process. By this he meant that they had their origin in creative processes of a practical nature, though the final result became nonobjective art. Some of them he regarded as pure abstract art but considered that, in contrast to what is usually the case with abstract art, they would perhaps sometime in the future come to some practical use. Perhaps he was right; I did not want to protest then and I won't do it now either. But as my personal and emotionally based insight I would like to add that architecture and its details are connected in a way with biology. They are perhaps like large salmon or trout. They are not born mature, they are not even born in the sea or a body of water where they will normally live. They are born many hundreds of miles from their proper living environment. Where rivers are but streams, small shining bodies of water between the mountains, under the glaciers' first melting water drops, there they are born, as far from their normal environment as man's spiritual life and instincts are from his daily work.

And as the fish egg's development to a mature organism requires time, so it also requires time for all that develops and crystallizes in our world of thoughts. Architecture needs this time to an even greater extent than any other creative work. As a little example from my own experience, I can tell about something that seemed like a game with form but after a long time unexpectedly resulted in a practical architectural form.

What is the evolution of the capital on an Ionic column? It has its source in the sculptural shapes of wood and the release of fibers under pressure. But the marble product is not a natural copy of this process. Its polished, crystalline shapes contain human elements that did not exist in the original structural form.

"Abstract art's universal characteristic is, in my understanding, its purely humane character." So a visiting painter reasoned at my drafting board. "I can't really explain it, but my intuition and experience tell me that it is so."

"Either I feel or I don't feel," a Swiss doctor said to me last summer, a man who had gone through the hard schooling of human tragedies. In this manner he expressed his personal atttude toward art.

Abstract art at its best is the result of a kind of crystallization process. Perhaps that is why it can be grasped only intuitively, though in and behind the work of art there are constructive thoughts and elements of human tragedy. In a way it is a medium that can transport us directly into the human current of feelings that has almost been lost by the written word.

This doesn't, of course, apply to the vulgar and commercialized forms of art that always thrive like weeds.

It would appear to me that we have already come a good way along the road to unity of the arts, and that unity can be traced in the lattice that unites the three branches of art at the roots, in their nascent form, not at the surface. It is obvious that we are at the beginning stage of this process toward unity, but this does not diminish its value. In the development of culture every epoch is artistically equal. From a human point of view we cannot place archaic art lower in our scale of values than the Acropolis. Giotto as a master was worth no less than his later colleagues in architecture and painting.

"Taimen ja tunturipuro," *Domus*, 1947

National Planning and Cultural Goals

Finnish culture, like everything in this world, is at times the subject of criticism, and in this criticism there are certain recurring features. One of them is this: a cross section of Finnish culture is too largely made up of literature; the fine and applied arts are not given the same weight. Not that they have been without accomplishments. On the contrary, we have received international recognition in many areas of our material culture. But in the average Finnish citizen's consciousness these areas don't play as big a role as those based on the alphabet, the values of the spoken and written word. This may be true or not, but in any case it means that too small a part of the cross section is left for such areas of culture as architecture (the art most deeply rooted in materials), for theoretical planning of cities and communities, for architecture's two older sisters, painting and sculpture, for the work of builders and engineers, for the inventor's technical creation, and finally for the art of design, whose goal is to give everyday objects a form that fits the tragedy and comedy in people's lives. We can even go so far as to include culinary culture, and so we have a whole group of cultural fields that in all likelihood will remain in the background when the popular mind projects its thoughts into cultural channels.

If this is so it cannot in any way be considered unnatural. One hundred years of Finnish cultural endeavor point in this direction. The Lönnrot-*Kalevala*[1] combination is in itself a literary point of convergence; in addition Lönnrot is probably the most sympathetic personality in our history—this strange gentleman, born in a poor farmhouse, who was an example of constant upward mobility that was never parvenu. Merely on the basis of such an authority one could say that normal thinking people in Finland are correct in sticking to our literary traditions.

Snellman[2] is a similar case, because, despite his practical disposition, what remains of his work deals primarily with

1. Elias Lönnrot (1802–1884) was the compiler of the *Kalevala*, the Finnish national epic.
2. Johan Vilhelm Snellman (1806–1881), Finnish philosopher, statesman, and nationalist.

literature and cultural linguistics. Then come the rise of the Finnish folk element, the popular educational efforts and the whole literature connected to them, right up to our day. Together all this forms a chain of events which explains why Finnish education presently has a literary orientation. There are no reasons why we should try to change this relationship by artificial means. Time will eventually leave its traces. But there is perhaps reason for us to make the effort to bring together these two main groups—literary culture and material culture, first because this will strengthen our culture and next because most of our areas of activity are such that we need support from both ends to achieve a happy result. Third, because there are hybrid art forms that have characteristics of both sides.

My main theme for today, national planning, belongs to this last category. It is a mixed form. National planning is such a comprehensive undertaking that the classical planning tools, pencils and prognoses, are not enough. A written program for national development is required, a program that can be only 50 to 80 percent based on planning. National planning as a phenomenon is a mixed form from another point of view. Because the program is directed toward the future it includes so many social and economic factors that it necessarily becomes something of a hybrid between a legal tome and a project. Finally, a planning project that affects the whole country must have a group of supporters. It must have people's conscious support, totally independent of whether these people are more interested in literary or material culture.

A national plan, a ready-made system for national guidance, presently exists only in one country. Switzerland has its so-called Landesplanung system, which was in operation long before the outbreak of the war. Somewhat similar projects exist however in other places as well. Our neighboring country, Sweden, has them; so has the Soviet Union, as far back as the five year plans. England's present government operates partly on county plans, and we ourselves have some partial, large-scale projects for certain historic areas. In this category, for example, are the general plans for the Kokemäenjoki and Kymijoki valleys. In these cases the basic plan is in existence; both are functioning fully. The administration is in the hands of a kind of inter-county office with civil servants who are developing the plan further and supervising its implementation.

These district plans naturally require that the project in question, instead of dealing with a small town, include larger areas. For example, in Pori there is a complete city planning office, but the Kokemäenjoki valley is purely rural with certain larger, densely populated areas. It does not offer the possibilities of a systematic effort of the type that a town can pursue within the boundaries of its master plan. If a true city planning effort is aimed, not only at one city but at a whole large area, as in the case of our country's oldest settled area, the Kokemäenjoki valley, then naturally whole new possibilities of benefit to the entire area are created. Industrial planning, for example, can be done to much greater benefit if it is not necessary to make a choice between one city and a rural area that can't offer the same advantages of legislation and experience.

Social planning in architecture involves a simultaneous solution for all functions—traffic, social questions, housing, industrial plants, aesthetic and commercial viewpoints, and many more, so that they become bound together into a unified network. Such simultaneous solutions should be formulated for larger areas if we are to achieve some order. Exactly as the medieval cities once upon a time lost their fortification walls and the modern city grew out beyond them, the concept of the city today is in the process of shedding its constraints. But this time it is happening, not to lead once again to the creation of a larger unit, but rather so that the city will become a part of the countryside. The underlying meaning of such regional plans is that they synchronize country and city.

National planning is essentially the same thing but on a larger scale. If all our river valleys gradually become so wealthy and culturally so developed that each one of them has its own regional plan, then naturally the different regions will develop their own internal communities of interest that can be coordinated wih one another. In this way a national plan gradually evolves. We have, in other words, the potential of adding on, piece by piece, district by district, gradually arriving at the point where a plan that encompasses the whole country is ready. There have also been attempts through legislation to set up a national planning office. I believe that the gradual path to development, one step at a time, building cell by cell, is the healthier. It is, after all, biology's and culture's own method of creation. By this path, the Finnish national plan would come about point by point, to grow gradually into a totality.

There are also other phenomena that can be regarded as having precedential significance and as preparing the way for national planning. The highway and waterworks administration's highway projects concern the whole country, as do the state railways' future plans. Even in agrarian reforms there are features that point to future national planning. By joining these different functions, by developing them further, for example, within regional borders, we will probably gradually create for ourselves a national plan.

Then we naturally arrive at the question that the doubter is tempted to pose. On the whole, is the modern tendency toward tighter and tighter planning necessary, and will it last? We must remembe that all projects are children of necessity. In a way the tight planning favored by our age is related to the development of industrialism. In itself it is not, just as industrialism's sharply rising curve is not, a liberating or creative instrument that is solely beneficial. Planning can even be harmful. Nearly all planning that is carried too far has a tendency to strangle and destroy life's natural forces. We all know Carrel's[3] theory about excessive medical care. It anesthetizes the automatic mechanisms that maintain the human body's balance. Precisely the same doubt is appropriate when we speak of the modern tendency to make everything in life conform to a pre-planned scheme.

Originally technology was a physical guarantee of freedom. The first house freed man from the vagaries of nature.

3. Alexis Carrel (1873–1944), French surgeon, biologist, and sociologist and winner of the Nobel Prize in medicine.

It was a clear sign of increased freedom. Man's first tools and weapons gave him a gradually increasing freedom of movement. And with physical freedom of movement follows psychic freedom. Since then technology has developed and freedom has been increased step by step. But when technological development reaches a certain point on the curve it no longer produces human freedom; other conditions arise, *and finally the same phenomenon that originally created people's freedom can become the factor that ties them down the most.* Let us think of modern developments that the big industries have brought with them in the larger countries. Huge, dense, unhealthy cities, a mass of social problems, an assembly-line mode of production that can, for example, make things so complicated that it requires thousands of interdependent hands for one single matchstick to find its way from the raw material stage to the consumer. Naturally, such a complicated production process leads to regulation, coercion, and the inevitable planning. Everything must be directed from an almost apical command point.

If national or town planning blindly follows a similar path, they will become harmful. *But planning can be carried out in another way. It can be regarded as an ethical means of development that puts a stop to centralization, leading where blind development cannot, and functioning as a guardian of ethics and human freedom.* If the large regional plan, or, let us say, the national plan, is built on such an ethical foundation, then it has made a good beginning.

Very recently certain strange phenomena have appeared. We speak of a flexible city plan, a consistently flexible instrument with which we would purposefully strive to increase freedom of movement and freedom even in other regards. For example, in an area like standardization, which is so tight and leaves so little room for maneuvering and restricts personal freedom to such a horrendous extent, there have appeared methods for so-called flexible standardization, which consciously strives to function as a counterweight to collectivization and exaggerated human controls, in other words, as a means to create freedom. It is not so easy to explain these means. They are often subtle and hard to grasp. Even a superficial explanation becomes complicated. One group of concepts is, however, such that I can briefly discuss it here. I am thinking of national planning's potential as a means of decentralization. In other words, there is a need for a force that works in the opposite direction, a force for decentralization. Within all major industrial companies, which in other parts of the world have become many times larger than here, there is always talk of the need for decentralization. One hears it in American auto companies and other similar industries. But there it is difficult to begin to implement decentralization, and it remains undone. In Finland, on the other hand, we could perhaps have a chance of finding the right path. To guarantee success we need a solid and clearcut tradition, a precedent. In Finland this happens to exist. Let me take an example from our own group of industrial companies, where the strange phenomenon of geographic decentralization occurred a long time ago and has already become a tradition.

If we visit a large Finnish factory, for example, a large cellulose factory, we see that it is as large an industrial unit as any equivalent factory in the big world. And yet it has not attracted masses of people and a clutter of settlements, nor does it collect innumerable social problems for coming generations. In the factory there are a few people, that is all. But Finnish cellulose requires as many hands for its production as Canadian cellulose. In fact there are thousands of working hands in this country, but not in the factory. The workers are located on the waterways, within widespread geographical areas. In other words, the factory's personnel are spread over an area of hundreds of kilometers. The region is not even populated exclusively by factory workers. A large proportion of the population is, for example, small farmers, which constitutes a link between the industrial worker and the farmer. This in itself is a remarkable phenomenon. And when we consider that the industry isn't located in a big city but along the shores of rivers and lakes, and that our metals industry has also undertaken decentralization according to the same principles, but hardly according to the same geographical im-

perative, then we can conclude that we have here practical and unique examples that do not exist in such a distinct form in any other part of the world.

If we expand the principles of national planning to include, for example, similar traditions, and carry them further, it is likely that we will achieve results that will maintain these favorable developments. But it could also be possible in our conditions to create model communities or a whole group of model communities that could serve as a prototype for other countries who want to study ways of breaking down the centralizing process into a decentralizing process and the social benefits to be derived. When I add that in Finland nature itself suggests, in a remarkable manner, a spread-out mode of settlement, we are approximately at the point where we began. I mean that perhaps we can consider the question of a common tradition in literary and material culture and the need to bring the two closer together. Finnish literature since the time of Lönnrot has been so close to nature that one hardly can find an exact equivalent anyplace else. If we take the *Iliad* and the *Kalevala*, the *Kalevala* is woven like a textile where every element is nature, constantly alive. The *Iliad* recounts objectively but leaves nature at that. This closeness to nature has been preserved in our literature until now (I am speaking not on a qualitative but on a quantitative basis) and closeness to nature outside of literature is a strong element in just about every average Finn's consciousness. I wonder if in the end we won't find a common bond for the literary and the material sides in this very closeness to nature. If we give national planning, city planning, and architecture a firm natural orientation, we will probably find a short cut to certain goals. Nature is, of course, freedom's symbol. Sometimes it is even nature that creates and maintains the concept of freedom. By giving our technical general plans a solid base in nature we can redirect the thrust of development in such a way that our daily work, in all its forms, increases our freedom instead of curtailing it.

"Valtakunnansuunnittelu ja kulttuurimme tavoitteet," *Suomalainen Suomi*, 1949

49. Fortification walls in Marrakesh, 1951
Landscape, Morocco, 1951

50. Sketch for the town hall at Säynätsalo, 1951

104

53. Cypresses, Morocco, 1951

108

Calascibetto. 52

110

Agrigento
52

The Decline of Public Buildings

The editor-in-chief of *Architectural Review* once sent me a letter asking me questions on many topics, among them monumentality and its position in today's architecture. It was a questionnaire, and many of my colleagues, whom I respect highly, had also been asked the same difficult questions. I informed the sender that I could not give my answer in writing; I would instead give it in buildings. But to answer with buildings is a time-consuming activity. The moment of attainment hasn't yet arrived. Despite this fact, there may be cause to touch on the problem briefly with a few words.

For my part, however, I would like to reformulate the question in such a manner that it fits under the title, "The Decline of Public Buildings." Because this decline is an unavoidable fact.

According to the time-honored European concept, a community's central areas were divided into two sections: residential quarters, whatever their character, all the way from slums to the houses of the aristocracy; and the areas common to all, for the proletariat just as much as for the senators. These, the public buildings, comprised the whole range from administrative palaces to the body of buildings within whose walls public activities were conducted in some form or other; government buildings to which everyone had access or was compelled to visit, communal institutions such as baths, libraries, and museums, and, naturally, all sacred places and areas. Among these one should, of course, include all open public places—squares, parks, and arcades where citizens, without differentiation, could gather, as well as public monuments and other similar symbols or formal narrative creations that were an integral part thereof. This order of things, which had been maintained in Europe through the ages, has now been shattered. The commercialism to which the French Revolution led, despite itself, in some respects, gradually created a new dominant element in the city, the commercial office building, which has since reached an enormous scale with which neither government nor the community building projects can compete.

But this building type hasn't inherited the public building's status in society or in town planning. Typically, this development reached its final form, not in France, but across the ocean in the Anglo-Saxon dominion and in America.

In this connection I am reminded of the many advances with which the Anglo-Saxon world has enriched society's form and character. These are definitely not insignificant. But they do not reflect the continental European culture's social pattern; public buildings do not occupy the same posiion as symbols, as institutions common to all people.

English colonization was based on the creation of settlements in parts of the world that often lacked the traditions for such an enterprise. The original center of these settlements was at times a modest common, which in the beginning had the same social significance as the public centers but which later became a kind of combination of public park and, for example, a football field. Around it the city developed as an amorphous mass, where commercial and residential areas underwent certain transformations while the community's public functions lost their thousand-year-old authority in the urban fabric. This is, of course, a generalization that doesn't hold up in all its details, but the difference between this new world and the continent's "sacred order" is so striking that one naturally asks oneself which world one really belongs to.

The question is perhaps superfluous. The transoceanic world's approach has made such gains that we in Finland, for example, have during the time of our independence built only a few public buildings of true authority. Our cities are also becoming, or have already become, amorphous masses where town halls, libraries, and other communal institutions, yes, even such a venerable institution as the Bank of Finland, are mere corner buildings on leased lots without the traditional imprint of government and the social contract. There is business space on the grond floor and a motley mixture of offices and dwellings on the upper floors. This system has become quite common with public buildings, putting them in the same category as ordinary office and apartment buildings.

And yet the position of public buildings in a community should be just as important as that of the vital organs in the human body if we want to prevent our communities from becoming psychologically repugnant and physiolog-ically destructive to their citizens. One can only hope that the manner in which our cities are presently being built is a transitional phenomenon. It certainly can't look to a particularly flattering critique from future generations.

Our communities must have a proper urban fabric.

Perhaps it is wrong to speak in terms of a reversion. A more adequate way of phrasing it would be to say that it is imperative to create anew the differentiation necessary for an organized community. The community that is now taking shape—it could be termed a classless society—is still more sensitive than bourgeois society, which the French Revolution created, because it encompasses larger masses of people whose physical welfare as well as civic and general cultural education is intimately dependent on the proper disposition of those institutions and spaces that serve the public life.

In our country the scale of things is still modest, and our social structure has continued to retain a certain adaptability that makes it possible for us to avoid the "main street" system and to create an organic approach to building, which allows public buildings and spaces their proper place.

This also has a profound implication for residential areas, wich cannot be developed into an organic totality if they are not organized so that local institutions have the same significance for these smaller neighborhoods that equivalent institutions at a larger scale have for major cities.

Neighborhood centers of this type have for a long time been one of the architect's chief goals. But finding a successful solution offers many economic problems. Nevertheless, one hopes that this path will open the possibility that a true differentiation will gradually emerge.

The planning of Helsinki's center is just in the process of taking shape. In conjunction with this event we have the possibility, even if limited, of giving Helsinki a center of public buildings that would correspond to the city's present size and needs. They are a great deal more complex today than a hundred years ago, when the capital last found its center in the Senate Square.

Arkkitehti-Arkitekten, 1953

Finland Builds:
Exhibition at the Ateneum, Helsinki

It is very difficult to characterize architecture's position in the Finland of today, because it is in many ways the most difficult of the arts to grasp and yet is at the same time so intimately tied to the everyday. Architecture should be of concern to everyone at least to the point of having some understanding of it. With the purpose of furthering the understanding of architecture in our country, the Finnish architectural profession has mounted a large exhibition in the Ateneum, a result of many years' work. It attempts to give an overview of the achievements of Finnish architecture during the past years. A total of 170 projects are displayed, which could be considered a unique accomplishment for any country in the world. It is uncertain whether such a large exhibition can be sent to tour the provinces, but in any event it will be shown abroad. For many years there has, in different parts of the world, been a desire to see a comprehensive exhibition of Finnish architecture. I have said architecture in general must be regarded as a difficult art to understand. It is an art intimately connected with materials. Architecture belongs to culture, not to civilization. To teach and popularize it is difficult and ineffective if done only with the help of words.

In reality the secure foundation for Finnish architecture is the so-called cultured Finland in the liberal sense of the term, which has an inherent feeling for art, an insight into it that is sufficiently deep so that no explanations are required.

Regardless of what position Finnish architecture has today in the world—and it isn't for me to take a position on the subject—it is at least certain that our architecture is not as well-known at home as it is beyond the country's borders. Our architecture does not have the position in the general public's consciousness that it must have if we are to succeed in building up our nation.

There wouldn't be any reason to demand special attention for architecture if it were not a field where mistakes are just about impossible to correct afterwards. How beautiful or ugly a country is depends on the level of its architecture, and to a still greater extent architecture affects the spiritual harmony and living standards of the country's inhabitants. Starting with basic education, which in this country doesn't concern itself at all with architecture, and through different popular media, it is imperative that we strengthen our cultural foundations in this area. Though Finland, when it comes to understanding architecture, is behind most civilized countries, one finds, on general inspection, that there are extenuating circumstances. I could mention, for instance, the exceptional architectural interest that our industries, especially the major industries, have shown. At a very early stage they applied aesthetic standards even to factory buildings. From this point of departure they have proceeded to the social sphere and created a pleasant working environment. We can only hope that this development will continue uninterrupted.

Quality of workmanship and the Finnish worker's contribution should especially be mentioned. In Finland it is possible, all criticism aside, to achieve quality on a level that is not usual in most parts of the world, and that has a direct positive effect on our architectural culture. This is noticeable both in industrial production and in individual efforts.

We have recently begun to encounter the Finnish worker more often in other connections, in administrative tasks, as a member of building committees. This same politically well-schooled worker, who, without leaving his ordinary workplace, is active in different administrative bodies, has become a dependable friend and a good supporter of architecture in Finland. We have seen men of this background handle chairmanships of committees and boards of large building complexes, and almost without exception they have supported good architecture with understanding.

Among the methods used to advance architecture there is one that is very popular in our country, the competition system. Relatively, Finland has more architectural competitions than any other country in the world, and even in absolute terms the number of such competitions has at times been greater in Finland than in other countries of whatever size. A competition implies a certain democracy in the sense that each entrant, even a young talent, has a chance. But the system's main task is, of course, to use the competition to help develop the profession's internal critique and maintain a high standard within architecture. The general public seems to take architectural competitions for granted. This is a very praiseworthy attitude, because the competition system is the only one that secures freedom of choice for different building projects and makes possible the weighing of different alternatives. The most remarkable thing is the sacrifice in terms of work that the country's architectural profession makes in this way. At the most 10 percent of the projects receive prizes. Thus the competition entries represent an enormous amount of labor whose effect on the country's cultural level is immediate and lasting.

Like everything else our architecture has its foes, a counterbalance to the understanding and support it receives. Its oldest archenemy has always been so-called building speculation. Only a few decades ago this speculative system flourished in Helsinki and others of our cities. The activity has markedly decreased in our day as a result of measures taken by our society and will no doubt be totally eliminated in time. Socially responsible planning of buildings will replace speculative building projects across the board.

An offshoot of the same speculative mentality is the opposition expressed, and the downright threatening behavior resorted to, by various elements recently in order to limit architecture's social and aesthetic values in favor of some type of economizing. Campaigns of this sort, however insignificant they may be, should be repudiated and opposed because they lead to the same type of slum formation as the speculative system. They have their source in the same interest groups. Interests hostile to architecture of the type just mentioned can best be countered through our society's own legislative actions and social purpose and through a general raising of the cultural level. This development is consistent with the enormous responsibility involved in fashioning nature and settlements in our country in such a manner that Finland may become a congenial home for each of us.

"Suomi Rakentaa Näytelly Ateneumissa," radio lecture, November 11, 1953

114

Experimental House, Muuratsalo

Ties of friendship usually unite people of the same generation. And yet I have counted among my truly close friends some who could be said to belong to the "grand old" generation, Helene de Mandrot, Henry van de Velde, Frank Lloyd Wright, and, in Finland, Yrjo Hirn.

Whether it is due to Yrjo Hirn's influence or not, through the force of his personality, a conception or an instinctive feeling has taken root in me, that we, in the midst of our hard-working, calculating, utilitarian era, must regard play as of decisive importance when we build communities for people—large children. This thought occurs in one form or another, I suppose, to every architect with a sense of responsibility.

To depend only on play, though, would become a game with form, structure, and finally with people's bodies and souls; it would be to take play too playfully. But Yrjo Hirn was serious, and he also took his theory of play with deepest seriousness. In a similar manner we should unite our experimental work with a play mentality or vice versa.

Not until architecture's structural elements, the forms logically derived from them, and our empirical knowledge are modified by what we seriously can call play, or art, will we be proceeding in the right direction. Technology and economy must always be combined with life-enriching charm.

On the high-lying island of Muuratsalo in the middle of Lake Paijanne, stands an experimental house—still without a name—which was built to give the architect a chance to play purely for pleasure's sake. But it has also been done for serious experimental purposes, essentially to deal with problems that the architect cannot get involved with on ordinary building projects. One should, of course, always experiment, even with one's clients' buildings, or there would be no progress either in architecture or building technology. And yet experiments can be given only the narrowest freedom of scope within the framework of practical requirements in a real building project. In our playhouse we* wanted to experiment even with things whose

115

*Aalto and his wife, Elissa.

practical content no one has yet measured.

The building complex at Muuratsalo is meant to become a kind of synthesis between a protected architectural studio and an experimental center where one can expect to try experiments that are not ready to be tried elsewhere, and where the proximity to nature can give fresh inspiration both in terms of form and construction. Perhaps it will be possible there to find the specific character of architectural detail that our northern climate requires.

The building has, with its experimental aim in mind, been designed so that it differs from the normal; the same forms have not been used throughout, nor the same scale, nor the same construction. Thus all the walls around the closed patio are divided into approximately fifty panels in which the effect of ceramic materials, brick, joints, different brick formats, and surface treatments have been tried out. These experiments with form also include tests of durability that are daily the object of the architect's observation. Similar experiments take place on the central patio, where from one year to the next we have tried different techniques for surfacing different areas, from the point of view of aesthetic effect. We have tried everything from brick and stone surfaces to decorative plants and mosses. The wall construction of the building varies, and for experimental purposes different roof constructions have been attempted.

Of the prospective building group the modest main house with its central patio is already finished, while the second building phase is currently in progress. This will include the following:

1. Experiments with a building without foundations, in this case, a diagonal system of beams laid on rocks embedded in the moraine ridge, so that the wood building has been stabilized despite the indeterminate location of the structural supports.

2. Experiments with an irregular row of columns (nonlinear colonnade) where the columns holding up the building have been placed in the most advantageous points in the terrain.

3. Free-form brick constructions. An attempt to develop a type of standard brick or standard element so that it be-comes possible to make walls in a capricious curved form without having to change the standard pieces, in other words, a sort of further development of the now practically forgotten form bricks, but adapted for other, more up-to-date purposes.

4. A studio that is not connected to the heating system of the other buildings crowns the group of buildings. This separate pavilion involves an experiment with solar heating such that wall and roof surfaces, which accumulate the warmth, are independent of the building's other parts. This is in contrast to what has been the practice in purely technical experiments up to this date.

The whole complex of buildings is dominated by the fire that burns at the center of the patio and that, from the point of view of practicality and comfort, serves the same purpose as the campfire in a winter camp, where the glow from the fire and its reflections from the surrounding snowbanks create a pleasant, almost mystical feeling of warmth.

Arkkitehti-Arkitekten, 1953

116

57. Stone floor or wall, Sicily, 1952

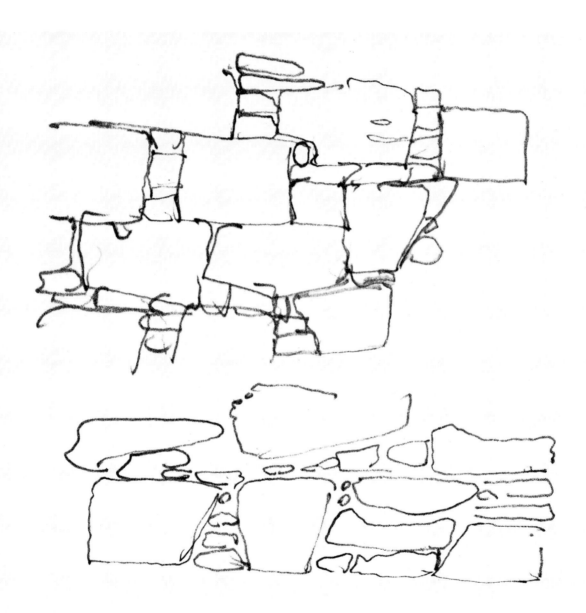

58. Arab village on the Euphrates seen from the air, 1954

118

59. View from an airplane. From a trip to Baghdad, 1954

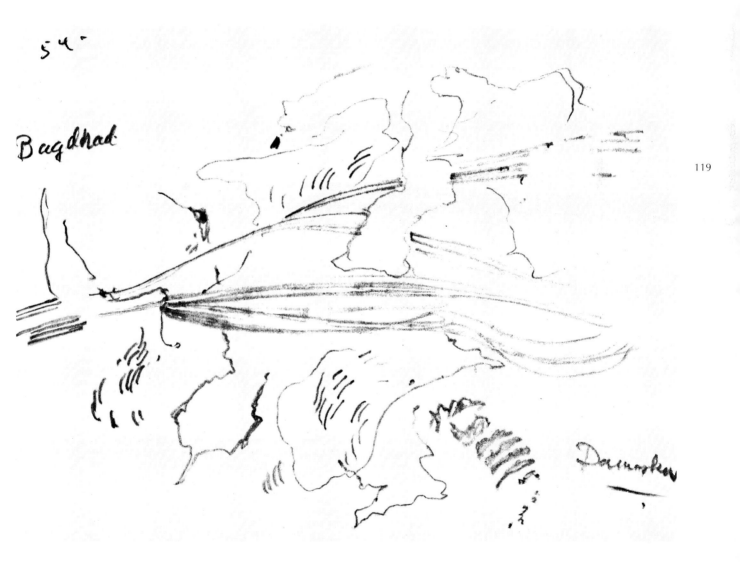

60. The God Thot from the temple at Luxor, Egypt, 1954–1955

120

61. Ships on the Nile between Luxor and Esna, 1954–1955

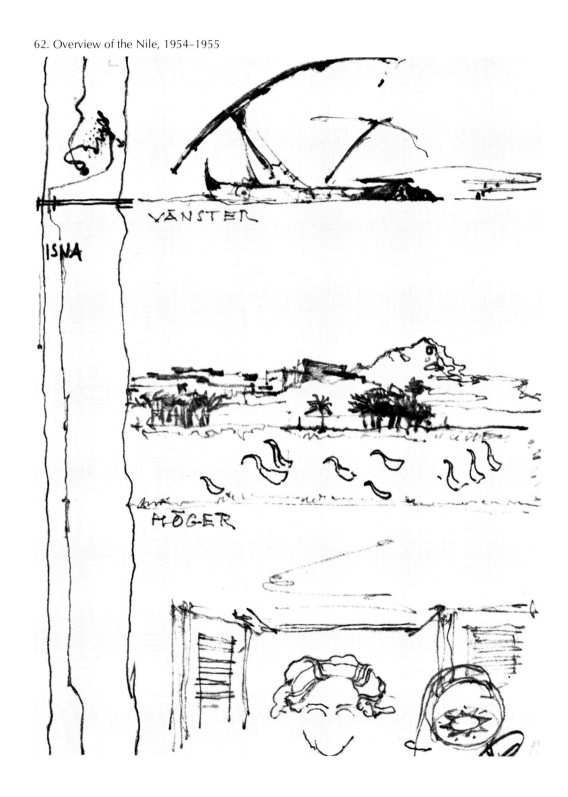

Art and Technology

When I have to deal with an intellectual conception that is mentioned in the title of my lecture (the internal relationship between art and technology) I am obviously faced with certain difficulties. It would be comparatively easy to sort out the concepts if I had at my disposal all the means I use in my daily work: sketches, line, color, constructions made up of different materials and buildings, but it is close to impossible to illuminate the whole of such a complicated problem with words alone.

The boundaries of art and technology are obviously not well defined. In the past these concepts were often considered the same thing or similar; different constellations of cultural significance appeared, according to whether it was a question of art, technology, handicraft, or whatever. Strictly speaking it is so even today within architecture, where the connection between art and technology is most obvious.

When we say that art is an element that controls or leads technology, whether it stands out separately or as an unseen ingredient that has combined chemically with the technical effort, we are also confronted with certain difficulties when it comes to explanation, especially in Finland. Ours is an era of sharp contrasts. The transition to a whole new life style, industrialism, has happened in a relatively short time, and certain constants, time-honored cultural forms, have been disturbed throughout the world, and obviously in our country as well. The country, the state, or some other grouping of people is both the field where the elements of creative work arise and, naturally, a receptor organ. And on just this circumstance, in other words, on how well the receptor organ functions, depends the case of clarifying the true basis of these problems.

We know that there are large areas of the world, in many countries, where the people's receptive capability is so low that they cannot even benefit from the culture that perhaps they themselves have created. There are countries where sometimes very forceful personalities are born but gradually disappear from their original milieu. Within different art forms we find many examples of creative talent gathered, let us say, in a European cultural center. There they are enjoyed by other nations while they themselves and the work they do are either totally or partly unknown in their native land.

What is Finland's situation in this respect? How is Finland as a recipient country? There are both good and bad things to say. But when it concerns art forms based on structure, in other words, architecture, sculpture, painting, and the forms of handicraft and technology (in a limited sense) that support them, then one has to say that a sampling in Finland does not produce a good result, not even a satisfactory one. The appreciation for these particular arts and for the connection between art and technology is weak, or at least not as developed as would be desirable.

This could be the result of many circumstances. Finland at the present stage of its educational development is in fact a country of a literary orientation. A whole hundred-year tradition has been strongly tied to literature and the written word. It is naturally easy to understand such one-sidedness in the land of the *Kalevala*, although Finnish folk poetry is actually related in a peculiar manner to art forms based on materials. Many talents, especially in architecture, painting, and music, have been inspired indirectly by this apparently purely literary source.

Naturally there are also other reasons that the general public's appreciation for and interest in the fields discussed are not as developed as for literature. It would appear that architecture's sister art, music, for example, enjoys greater receptivity and understanding. I am not altogether sure if I'm correct on that point. Both music and architecture are, as we know, based on the mathematical dimension, on the type of mathematics that, from an international point of view, no longer appears to be mathematics. They are both bound to impulses originating in materials. Music is impossible without the phenomenon of vibration in matter, both living and dead. But at a time when the rootless music of entertainment, which travels entirely on popularity's paths, seems to have drowned out music of real quality, it is possible that I exaggerate when I say that appreciation for music in Finland is greater than appreciation for architecture and the visual arts, which belong to the same

sphere and grow in the same manner out of materials shaped by technology.

I could continue on this theme. Even the existence of two languages in Finland, as enormously useful as it has been in many respects for the country, must bear a part of the blame at least for the fact that popular understanding of architecture is weak. The turn-of-the-century Swedish literature on architecture was not, as far as I'm aware, sold in large Finnish editions, not to speak of the fact that it had no influence in the provinces.

There are, of course, many other reasons. Sometimes they may appear to counteract each other, and they can even have a positive influence. It has been claimed that the lack of knowledge of architecture and the weak appreciation for architecture in general that have existed in certain circles in Finland have on the whole acted as a smoke-screen, behind which the art has developed. It has not been subject to any inhibiting pressure, the result of, for instance, an older culture, such as is always present in France, where it has often stood in the way of new forms.

However, it should be said that a protective system of this type cannot produce a living culture. It is always to the general advantage that all activity within a cultural field be conscious or that it be included, to as great a degree as possible, in the popular consciousness. One can hardly imagine that valuable achievements carried out in the shadow of ignorance, or some kind of semi-culture, would indicate an independent and developing civilization.

Lack of knowledge and a lack of appreciation alongside excellent accomplishments—here we certainly have a strange contrast. And there are many other contrasts in the picture of the Finnish people. To a certain extent this is the case with most groups of people. Sometimes one can, among totally ordinary people, find a remarkably deep insight, and alongside of it just as unexpectedly an almost total blindness and indifference to something that is part of a more or less similar phenomenon. This is the case, for example, with understanding our formal environment, of what the inhabited world should be like during our time here on earth. In a refined form, people's surroundings, everything they have built up or created from matter during their lifetimes, is in reality matter ennobled by art, or, to say it in a more modern way, matter refined by art and technology. Precisely on this point the cultural variations in Finland are surprising and extreme. Popular understanding of art, for example, is still for the most part at a fairly low level. The general level of education achieved during the last decades of the nineteenth century has in some way separated art from the whole physical world around us. There is a great deal of interest in art in our society. However, this interest manifests itself in different ways. There are those who consider collecting some type of art work all that is necessary to be taking an active part in cultural affairs. They see an appreciation for an isolated group of art objects as a sufficient contribution for a person or a group. This involves, of course, isolation from our proper environment. For a person with this attitude it is naturally of no consequence how the organic structure that surrounds him evolves: he does not care what his home village looks like, how the city he lives in is structured or functions, if it improves on or destroys nature, if the traffic flows smoothly or if it is a free-for-all, just to name a few examples.

And yet the true sign of culture is the ability to create a balance in the whole environment of cities, villages, traffic arteries, nature, and other elements that form the framework of our lives, and only in this totality can one include true art and the refined types of technology that serve man in a proper way. A conception of art that is based, for example, on one branch of the visual arts is incomplete and prejudicial to the whole. One realizes this if one keeps in mind that the most important thing is always how the whole community is formed, what we make with our own hands of the material through which our lives are finally to be channeled.

During the transition in our culture that is now taking place we see an extreme and immature nostalgia for questionable forms of semiculture and banality, a Hollywood transplanted to the wilds of Finland, and, alongside this,

sprouted with dramatic suddenness, certain clever attempts at solutions that aim at human happiness and a correct design of the environment. Tragedy and comedy alongside superficiality and unexpected depth—this is the melting pot that contains the ingredients of the coming society.

If we think about these dizzying contrasts under whose sign we live we find that a summary account hardly does them justice. One would perhaps like to call on the help of poetry, some Strindbergian expression for irreconcilable contrasts.

Goldpower at the ironspring
Coppersnake under silver linden
that is the lady of the wood's riddle
that is yours and mine.

By this Strindberg probably means that apparently irreconcilable opposites may at last in one way or another be brought into harmony. Another poet: "Only high poetry can deal with any and all motifs and create harmony: just a little lower down the vulgar remains vulgar." But Strindberg's way of placing the opposites next to each other in any case hints at the manner in which art and the purely material world may be united.

Whatever our task may be, big or little, with its source in everyday ugliness or the most fragile feelings, a city or a part thereof, a house, a traffic network, or perhaps a painting, a sculpture, or a simple utilitarian article, there exists an absolute condition for creative work, if the result is to reach a level that makes it culture. There is more than this one condition but we will begin with it.

In every case one must achieve a simultaneous solution of conflicting problems. A modest example: An ordinary brick is for all appearances a primitive product, but if it is made correctly, properly processed from the country's own raw materials, if it is used in the right way and given its proper place in the whole, then it constitutes the basic element in mankind's most valuable and visible monuments and is also the basic element in the environment that creates social well-being. Another example: Let us say that our purpose is to build a church. The nature of the foundation, the geographical and local siting, the building materials for walls and roof, heating system, ventilation, lighting, and surface treatment, and innumerable other factors are basically independent of each other. Fundamentally these are independent problems, and as parts of the church structure they are often even in conflict with one another, and yet it is necessary to bring them into harmony. Only if and when this harmony is achieved does the building become a cultural factor of permanent value to the society, and only in conflict-free unity do these factors create a temporal continuity.

Nearly every design task involves tens, often hundreds, sometimes thousands of different antagonistic elements, which can be forced into a functional harmony only by man's will. This harmony cannot be achieved by other than artistic means. The individual technical and mechanical elements receive their definite value only in this manner. A harmonious result cannot be achieved via calculations, or with the help of statistical data or probability calculations.

New methods are constantly appearing which claim to make it possible to achieve this totality through calculations and laboratory tests. Within a relatively short period they are forgotten. To this category also belongs the method of deciding dwelling patterns purely by economic calculations. The economic point of view is primary in our work. Even here economics is a good guiding star when it is necessary to decide on the limits within which we can maneuver. But people cannot be formed by a one-sided calculation. It becomes uneconomical in the long run.

There are statistically based methods and some kind of Gallup system with whose help it has been attempted to achieve a harmonious whole. There is, for example, an enormous hospital, recently built, based on the movement patterns of the staff, in the hopes of simplifying the bio-dynamic movements of the people working in the building. The results have shown themselves to be totally unsuccessful. It was an attempt to achieve a total solution relying on a subordinate factor.

As a teacher I once heard a student present his thesis project. It concerned a children's hospital. He had attempted to find the overall solution not only through one secondary method but through many. The analysis of movement patterns took half an hour of the speaker's time. There were the space needs for children of different ages, different light angles in the window systems, easy maintenance of surfaces, etc. All of them good things in themselves if one understands them as subordinate elements, but they were in this case not sufficient to create a humane environment or a functioning whole. When the student had finished counting up all these methods and presented his technical solutions for all the cases, I could not help but say: You have apparently still left out at least one possibility. How would the building and the sick children in it function if a wild lion jumped in through one of the windows? Would the dimensions be suitable in such a case? The answer was a deep silence in the whole auditorium. Only the laugh of the experienced pediatrics professor from Harvard could be heard.

In addition to the simultaneous solution there is another, perhaps even more important, factor: the human scale, in other words, the right proportion in everything we do. It has been claimed that architecture in recent times has found its own path and its own ancient task, even if in a new form, as some kind of humanizing force within an essentially mechanized sphere. We have dreamed of being master of the machine, not its slaves. This cannot be done by literary means; it requires an art based on materials that understands its task correctly. If we omit man from our work, whether it involves art or technology, how can we then protect "the little man" in today's mechanized world? It is not enough that he be protected on the level of ideology. Technology, even the more vulgar forms of technology, must in each detail practice the same synthesis: think of man above all.

It is not always easy to protect "the little man." Just one example before I end. We all know what we mean by standardization. It is one of technology's most effective means of realizing a form of present-day democracy, to spread useful things over a much larger area than has previously been possible. But while this standardization works to the benefit of the masses, it contains a seed of destruction if it is misused. We often dream of a dwelling in the same way as, for example, of a car. It is very common to strive for a kind of standard solution and through it a solution to the housing question. But if we compare the task of the standard product (the car) with that of a person's home (a house), we easily see that we are dealing with different quantities.

The car's task is to transport people from one place to another. It stands on four wheels and always in the same environment, in other words, on a highway or street. Dwellings, on the other hand, exist in millions of different places with constantly varying characteristics; sometimes the sun is here, sometimes there; in other words, the points of the compass change, as well as the landscape, the human well-being factor, and the disturbing elements in the environment; traffic arteries flow on different sides of the house or housing area; dwellings are built at different latitudes, from the Spitzburgs to the tropics. And people themselves vary. They are not objects. They are living beings; they have families, they have many different kinds of occupations. In other words, their environment cannot easily be standardized, as is true for a mechanical object. It requires new and better methods; vulgar technology is not enough. And at the same time one of civilization's basic problems demands a solution: How can the mass production of necessities be broadened in scope without detriment to people's natural individuality and the natural variations in their surroundings? The house and the community should in other words be built with people's lives and need for harmony in mind. So-called flexible standardization actually exists. I would like to call it humane standardization.

When speaking of standardization one of course begins to think of its international context—the same products, the same types, and the same forms spread over the whole world from Helsinki to Detroit, Moscow to Istanbul. At first it seems hard, almost impossible, to withstand the coming of such an international infiltration of standard objects. In technology's most primitive sphere the goal has already been reached. It should be said, however, that a totally rootless, airborne internationalism, even though its products may be the results of careful research, perhaps still doesn't offer the right opportunity to create a technological

object in cases where man and his ward, art, are the decisive factors.

International uniformity still perhaps doesn't succeed in creating culture despite the fact that the first achievements seem very promising. Large laboratories, giant laboratories with which we cannot compete almost force the Finnish scientist to his knees. And yet, perhaps there is a possibility even for a small country to find its program. Even art, especially art, must in one way or another establish itself firmly in the changing envionment I talked of earlier. An amorphous mass cannot keep it alive. Perhaps we will find a solution by which art with roots in a certain national milieu can at the same time be relevant to a wider field. Of course I don't mean that we should design our cities, our houses, and objects, according to folkloric precedents or language divisions. But there is a deeper, perhaps mystical domiciliary right for thought and work which builds upon the popular psyche and on purely geographic conditions. The possibility ccurs to one that such a small country as Finland could be used as a kind of laboratory to produce on a small scale things that the larger nations cannot make in their giant laboratories. Such a possibility exists, especially in the matter of the human environment: the shaping of cities, the countryside, dwelling complexes and units with dimensions of human proportion. To this could be linked the manufacture of finished products, and experiments would aim at testing the articles' suitability for "the little man."

This whole field lies in some way beyond the large laboratory's task; it is nonimperialistic. Or at least this form of activity could not spawn projects close to the heart of the world centers for mass production. It should be possible to make of a small country a laboratory for people's intimate environment, their way of living, and related cultural forms. But this presupposes that the phenomenon I first talked about, people as an impulse-giving and creative factor, and at the same time as receptive instruments, is highly developed.

129

"Taide ja tekniikka," lecture given upon his installation in the Finnish Academy, October 3, 1955

Between Humanism and Materialism

It is a great pleasure for me to speak for the first time here in Vienna to you, dear colleagues and friends, and to you ladies and gentlemen. Naturally this is not the first time I have been to Vienna. As a young architect, still wet behind the ears, I, like so many other Finnish architects, chose Vienna as the destination of one of my early study trips. The architectural curriculum in our small corner of Scandinavia has been strongly influenced by Viennese thinking, to such a degree that even today when students at the technical university in Helsinki wish to make fun of a certain professor they start with "Otto Wagner said. . . ."

The long battle, which was to a large extent fought in Vienna, was necessary to bring architecture into line with today's needs. This we all know, and we also know that there is no perceptible end to the battle, that it must continue, as we are confronted by one new problem after another.

I am convinced that the time-honored architectural tradition of Vienna will live on in the future and will constitute a key factor in solving our most difficult problems.

At times the problems of architecture are perceived on a very superficial level, as exemplified by the question put to a traveler arriving in New York: "Are you modern or conservative?" Things are seen from too formal a point of view. The most difficult problems are not encountered in the search for a form for modern life, but rather in the attempt to create forms based on true humanistic values. We know that we are living in an era of continual struggle against mechanization and machines.

An example of this struggle against the excessive mechanization of the world is Charlie Chaplin's film *Modern Times*. The same attitude may be found in literature and the theater. We declare ourselves the masters of machines when in reality we are their slaves. This paradox reflects one of architecture's greatest problems.

It is absolutely clear that architecture, following its period of modern formalism, is now faced with new tasks. Perhaps the architect is in a better position than the writer to give man superiority over the machine. In any case, the architect has an obvious task: to humanize the characteristics of building materials.

If we study this conflict more closely we arrive at the fundamental problem, that man apparently cannot create without at the same time destroying.

Not only ever-increasing mechanization but also our own actions estrange us from nature. We see how road construction destroys nature to a certain extent. And on closer inspection we find similar phenomena in all branches of the architectural profession. We have created, for example, better and better forms of artificial lighting. Our electric light is much more practical than our grandfathers' oil lamps or wax candles. But is the quality of this light really better than what we obtained from the old sources? In fact it is no better at all. Nowadays we use a sixty- to eighty-watt lightbulb when we wish to read at a certain distance from the light source. Our grandparents managed with two candles. Even incandescent light is no longer good enough: high-intensity fluorescent lights have been introduced which give an inconstant light with excessive amounts of blue. We are using more light for the same task as before, because the physical and psychic qualities of the light are no longer satisfying. The same phenomenon exists everywhere. I hesitate to mention the observed fact that ventilation through metal ducts is thoroughly impractical. For years we have known that the best ingredient in the air, ozone, disappears on account of the friction that arises in the ducts. Laboratory tests have in fact proved that the biologically active elements of air almost completely disappear as a result of the rapid mechanical pumping of air into office buildings. We pump air into the poor typist but only a small fraction is of use to her. It keeps her alive, but not much more. Nobody thinks of her physical well-being.

I have touched upon a few problems that leave a peculiar aftertaste. However, we are all aware that such inhuman and unnatural conflicts exist everywhere.

The architect's task is to restore a correct order of values.

I shall now show you a few pictures, but I cannot give very typical examples of the conflicts I have described. We can, I suppose, increase the level of humanism in the world only to a limited degree. For one man or even ten, not even a hundred active artists can totally transform it. With the aid of pictures I would like to illustrate a few of the instances where we are on the borderline between humanization and mechanization. These projects are my own, since, as a practicing architect, I feel the risk of criticizing my colleagues. I think it is obvious that the only possibility is to allow the architectural results to speak for themselves rather than to theorize.

The first slide I show here is a typical picture of my country. Its purpose is to give you an idea of the landscape that surrounds the buildings I shall discuss. It is a land of forests and lakes, over 80,000 lakes. The people have always been able to maintain their contact with nature in this land. The cities are small, the capital having only 400,000 inhabitants, the next largest town approximately 100,000. Cities with 30,000 inhabitants are considered medium-sized, and such a city may well be an administrative center. Everyone can live at the water's edge along the countless lake shores and enjoy the pleasures of pine forests and fresh waters. In reality, of course, this is not so, life isn't that simple and people cannot always settle wherever they please. Everything must, of course, be properly organized.

And now I will show a series of pictures of one of my old projects. This is a project during which I came in contact for the first time with human misfortune. The project in question is the Tuberculosis Sanatorium in Paimio. When I received the assignment I was myself ill and therefore had the opportunity to make a few experiments and find out what it really felt like to be sick. I became irritated at having to lie horizontal all the time, and my first observation was that the rooms were designed for people who are upright and not for those who lie in bed day in and day out. Like moths to a lamp my eyes were constantly drawn to the electric light in the room, which was absolutely not designed for bedridden patients. The room conveyed neither balance nor calm. I therefore decided to plan the patients' rooms in such a manner as to provide a restful atmosphere for the bedridden patient. I did not use, for example, artificial ventilation, which causes a disturbing draft about the head, but designed a system that draws warmed air from double-paned windows.

This is just one example of how we can do our little bit to alleviate people's suffering. Another example is the washbasin. I tried to design a washbasin where the running water makes no noise. The water hits the porcelain at an acute angle and therefore doesn't disturb the patient lying nearby.

I shall now make a quick jump from the sanatorium to a university that lies a little farther to the north. The main university building includes a library, sports facilities, a gymnasium, and a large school. We all know that modern education is highly collectivized. Nowadays we can more or less educate our children only according to a uniform system, and we can no longer speak of any individuality in educational methods. We know that collectivity has its good sides, but it can also be harmful. Somewhere between absolute individualism and total collectivism there must exist a happy medium. Schools are becoming larger and larger because this reduces the cost of administration. But a school should also have a maximum limit on its size. This is quite an ordinary primary school that serves a pedagogical institute for both teachers and students. In general, school buildings are much too big and the system of many classes is dictated by an extreme collectivization. Instead of one large school with many classes, I attempted to design a group of many small schools. Three classrooms and a stair landing together form a separate entity so that the illusion of a small school is created—a school that is administratively a part of the whole complex.

Here you see the plan for a crematorium. We have already discussed the less pleasant effects of school collectivization. There is also another type of organized human activity that can seem very offensive. It is terrible to visit a well-organized crematorium in a city with many million inhabitants. Corpses have to be searched for with the help of an alphabetical list. In such a situation the system should function so as not to offend anyone's feelings. According to the program for this particular crematorium a certain number of ceremonies took place each day. To put it bluntly, the chapel had to have a certain capacity. This led to a situation where different ceremonies could get in each other's way. I therefore attempted to design a plan that guaranteed that clashes could be avoided. Thus we have a large chapel here, a smaller chapel there, and an even smaller one here, each one with its own entrance. Different ceremonies can thus proceed independently of each other.

I have a feeling that there are many cases in life where the organization of things is experienced as too brutal. The architect's task is to make our life patterns more sympathetic.

You now see a new technical university twenty kilometers from the center of Helsinki. On the approach to the university from the city, avenues of old trees lead up to the main building, the laboratories, the faculty housing, the student housing, and the sports center. The footpaths have been arranged so that a professor, for example, can walk from his house to the lecture building without being forced to cross a roadway. Cars travel at the periphery of the campus, so that only parks separate the various buildings. Cars have become a permanent part of our life, but they must travel other roads; in other words, they require their own zones just as people working or at leisure require theirs. It is important that the zone designated for people at work or at rest should be at a level above the car zone. We know that fuels such as gasoline produce fumes that affect the human body. This may be an explanation for the occurrence of cancer. Although we have no proof of this, no expert would dare to contradict this statement with certainty. It is tragic that the conveniences of modern life conceal great hazards that constitute an unavoidable threat to the working person. This technical university is no more than an amateurish effort to solve some of these problems. But clearly it is an advantage that traffic is directed around the outside of the complex, that the green areas are grouped in among the buildings and that the dwellings are raised above the ground level; one can perhaps claim that the air there is less polluted by noxious fumes than elsewhere.

The university has an extensive sports area for the students and a large hall where different summer sports can be pursued during the winter. Personally I'm against sports becoming universalized so that summer is turned into winter and winter into summer. I think that one should pursue a sport and change it according to the time of the year so that one may experience the natural changes of the seasons. Javelin throwing indoors is not as noble a sport as javelin throwing outdoors in the woods or by the shore. In an indoor swimming pool or an ice hockey arena the seasons are changed de facto and a person's leisure activities have been divorced from nature.

It is reasonable that I should devote the remainder of my talk to another aspect of architecture, to form. Although the solving of architecture's problems is tied to the necessary process of humanization, we are still left with the old problem of monumentality and form, unchanged. All attempts to eliminate it would be as fruitless as trying to take the idea of heaven out of religion.

Although we know that wretched mankind can hardly be redeemed no matter how we try, yet it is still the architect's duty to attempt to humanize the age of machines. But this should not be done without regard for form.

Form is a mystery that defies definition but gives people a feeling of pleasure totally different from anything accomplished with government aid. Therefore I would like to close my lecture with a few thoughts on form.

Brick is an important element in the creation of form. I was once in Milwaukee together with my old friend Frank Lloyd Wright. He gave a lecture that began, "Ladies and gentlemen, do you know what a brick is? It is a small, worthless, ordinary thing that costs 11 cents but has a wonderful quality. Give me a brick and it becomes worth its weight in gold." It was the first time I had heard an audience told so bluntly and expressively what architecture is. Architecture is the turning of a worthless stone into a nugget of gold. In Finland we have certain difficulties with this process of transformation.

My associates and I have tried to establish an experimental house to encourage the process. We have built many experimental walls with different types of bricks and we have been able to communicate with the bricks each time we stay in the house, for it is always easier to discover brick's qualities in untouched surroundings. We have also examined the effects of plants on a brick wall. For an architect it is a shock suddenly to see yellow lichen creeping out over the stone; and however small the plants may be, they are stimulating.

I was once asked, "Why don't you do more free-form designs like the New York Pavilion?" The man who asked was an aesthete. "I have not had suitable building materials," I replied.

We cannot create a free-form architecture with standard elements. A rectangular brick is not suitable. The brick wall will retain its rectilinearity until a brick is invented that allows for freedom of form. It must be possible to find a form for a brick wall that is round, convex, concave, right-angled, everything.

When I speak here in Central Europe, where the form brick was invented, it is perhaps fitting to say in conclusion that we still do not by any means have the right building materials for the architectural forms we need. It is not just the brick that should have a universal form suitable for everything; the same is true of all forms of standardization.

When we have reached the stage where we can achieve different ends with one and the same standard unit, which elastically adapts itself to its task, then we shall have forced the passage between Charybdis and Scylla, between individualism and collectivism.

"Between Humanism and Materialism," lecture given at the Central Union of Architects in Vienna, 1955

133

65. Perspective, Baker House, Massachusetts Institute of Technology, Cambridge, Massachusetts, 1947

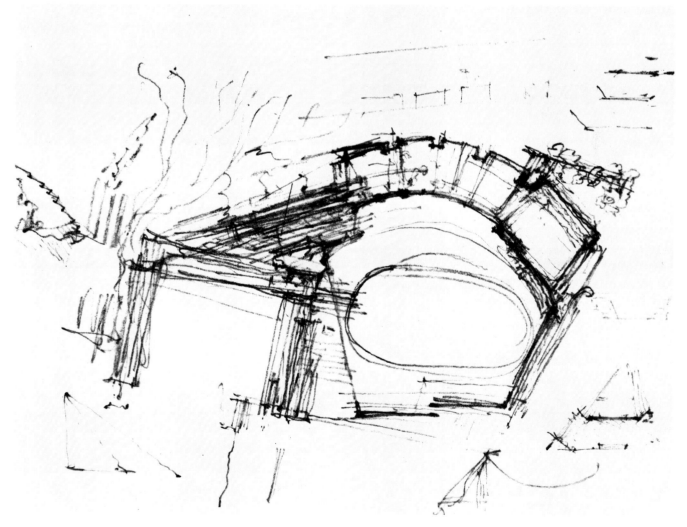

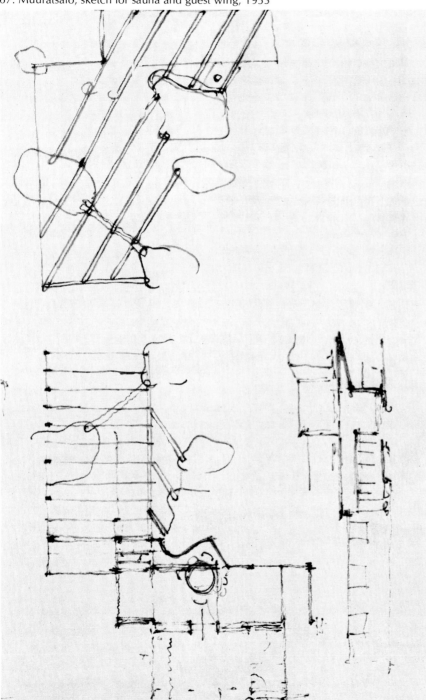

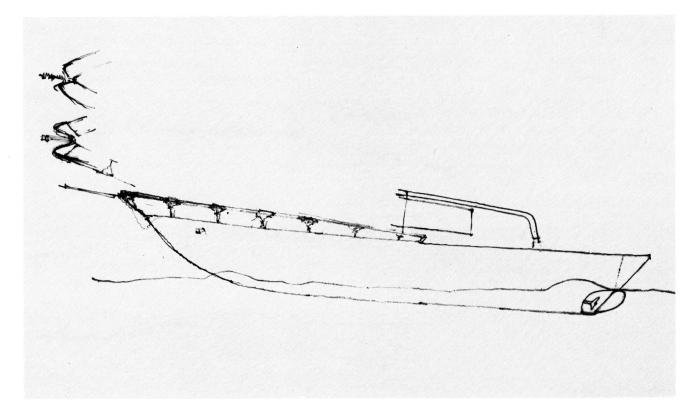

138

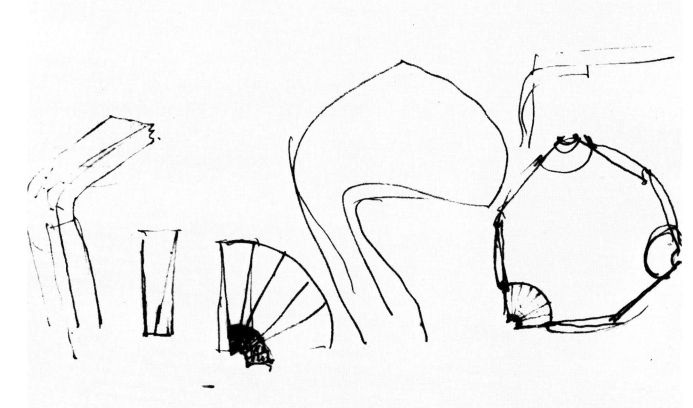

70. Organ in Seinäjoki church, c. 1958

Wood as a Building Material

When investigating the origin of primary architectural forms, one usually refers to wood and the ease with which it can be processed. In almost all cultures an architecture of wood has been the point of departure for later methods of construction and served as an experimental field for a whole form culture. Wood as the dominant element of architecture is essentially most common in the northern latitudes and similar climates. Despite this limitation its prevalence around the world is enormous. Another factor is the rich variety of woods and their workability. Therefore the role of wood today is hardly less important than during antiquity when the prototypes for the sculpted columns, the architectonic system of joists, and ornamental motifs in stone had been developed in an older wood architecture. One of wood's basic characteristics has, in our own time, become of decisive importance: its ease of transport. Factory-made building elements and prefabricated houses have, if we look at the better results, been of wood construction or of materials developed from wood.

Wood's biological characteristics, its limited heat conductivity, its kinship with man and living nature, the pleasant sensation to the touch it gives, as well as the possibilities of various types of surface treatments it offers, have all secured it a dominant position in architectural interiors, despite all recent experiments in other directions.

At the same time wood's drawbacks, its flammability and need for upkeep, have decreased its importance as a structural element and as a facade material. It has become increasingly valuable as a material for light roof construction with large spans, thereby increasing the possibilities for variations in architecture's already rich world of forms.

Wood will no doubt maintain its position as the most important material for sensitive architectural details. The synthetic materials that copy wood have in this regard not been able to replace it. In the chemical process upon which the synthetics are based, certain of wood's original and most important—and psychologically very valuable—characteristics are lost, which means that in all likelihood wood will retain its position as the form-inspiring, deeply human material whose resources are far from exhausted.

Arkkitehti-Arkitekten, 1956

Henry van de Velde
in Memoriam

Henry van de Velde, the European continent's grand old man in terms of revitalizing the arts, was one of the earliest links in the chain of development which has led to architecture's creative role in our social system.

When he passed away van de Velde was close to 95 years old. This alone is a proof of his creative vitality, which reached its peak beyond the age that is usually considered to mark the limits of physical survival. From the period of Art Nouveau to our own epoch is a time span that encompasses a great deal more than the number of years would indicate. It is of immense importance that during a period of rapid transition, when so much has happened, one person and his oeuvre have been able to trace such a mighty arc.

Even van de Velde's earliest works emanate a special charm. He did not have Art Nouveau's early years to himself. An excursion through the epoch's architectural production in Europe becomes a fantastically rich trip through time. Its buildings are often small ones, hidden in the mass of the turn of the century's voluminous output. They do not represent, as we have long been led to believe, a form of decoration as an end in itself; rather they hint in a remarkable way of something organic, the first hints of innovations from which we still benefit. It is an epoch that can be likened, let us say, to Giotto's, the spiritual and Dante-shadowed atmosphere of the pre-Renaissance.

143

This is not the place to list van de Velde's buildings or his contributions to various cultural fields. Let it be said simply that his personal influence has penetrated deeply into the Nordic countries; in Finland it is most strongly represented by Sigurd Frosterus. The intellectualization of architecture, that exceptionally healthy feature which was represented in our country by Sigurd Frosterus and Gustave Strengell, can be traced to van de Velde.

What the van de Velde era indirectly has meant is not clearly measurable, but it is conceivable that a considerably coarser and probably more vulgar character would have been evident in our architecture if a continental injection from him and his time had not influenced developments in a more cultivated direction.

Arkkitehti-Arkitekten, 1957

The RIBA Discourse: "The Architectural Struggle"

Our time is full of enthusiasm for, and interest in, architecture because of the architectural revolution that has been taking place during these last decades. But it is like all revolutions: it starts with enthusiasm and it stops with some sort of dictatorship. It runs off the track. There is one good thing that we still have today; we have all over the world, in Uruguay, in Scandinavia, in England, in South Africa—in all these countries—well-organized groups of creative people calling themselves architects, with a new, real—what should I say?—direction in the world. Slowly, from being formal artists, they have moved over into a new field; today they are the *garde d'honneur*, the hard-fighting squadron for humanizing technique in our time. With a client in Paris, a few days ago, I had a discussion about just such a simple thing as ventilation. He said, "Technique *sans esprit* is the worst thing in the world"—which it is.

Let us see how we do this work. Are we doing it right? Let us take two poles. If I arrive at Grand Central Station, or a station in Chicago, and some of the young architects are there, the first question—if they do not know me—is, "Are you old-fashioned or modern?" I have heard this question in all civilized languages and lastly in Portuguese, in Estoril. I think this is probably the most naïve but the most used formula—"Are you old-fashioned or modern?" If we look deeper into this question, we see just why it is nonsense and nothing more.

There are only two things in art—humanity or its lack. The mere form, some detail in itself, does not create humanity. We have today enough of superficial and rather bad architecture which is modern. It would be hard to find any architect able to design a Gothic or Georgian detail today.

Let us take some capital of entertainment—Hollywood, for instance. Of course all the houses are modern. But you can find very few houses that give human beings the spirit of the real physical life.

Let us take the other pole. A few months ago an Indian architect went to snow-covered Finland—I think he was from Bombay or New Delhi—and he had a book in which he had written all the questions that are the most important in the building art. Sitting down, he asked the first thing, after saying "How do you do?"—"What is the module of this office?" I did not answer him, because I did not know. One of my chief lieutenants was sitting on my right. He answered. He said, "One millimeter or less."

These are two poles that demonstrate first the pendulum of the most popular forms of discussion, and then this last one, this nonsense number two—the search for a module should cover all the world. This represents at the same time the dictatorship that finishes the revolution, the slavery of human beings to technical futilities that in themselves do not contain one piece of real humanity.

How should we carry on our fight? In what way? What should be the real intercommunion between all the architects of the world, and what should we tell the public? The Institute of Finnish Architects, a few days ago, left at the Secretariat General of the International Union of Architects in Paris a suggestion that we should name the obstacles that keep the good products back, say why so few cities are well planned, why so many good city plans are turned down, why there is so small a percentage of good housing, and why in our time we almost lack official buildings, which are symbols of the social life, symbols of what may be called democracy—the building owned by everybody.

The reasons that culture stops at the line of 2 percent, 4 percent, or 5 percent of the whole are, of course, deep and very difficult to analyze. That is the question of our time; it is a question of the deeper meaning of civilization and culture, a question of the movement from, let us say, the society of 1700 to our industrialism. Every piece today is made by different methods from those used before. Our life has taken on a completely different form. This must, of course, hurt; it cannot be a painless transition. There are, of course, obstacles to more good products; but there are things that can be eliminated by goodwill, and if we study them I think we should get a larger share of good things for the little man in this democracy of today.

I would add one thing more: there should be discussion on a broad basis. There is today a tendency that is not very nice. There are exhibitions of architecture and of industrial art or arts. There are hundreds of these exhibitions, organized not only here but on the Continent. The journalists say, "Today Sweden is a leading country in glass; tomorrow, Finland is a leading country in glass, this country is leading in pottery, Brazil is leading in colored façades." I do not think this is the correct way. We should put all the cards on the table and speak together, plan together, and openly talk about our weaknesses. We should not be like puppets and say, "Yes, we are leading in glass today."

We should remember the great eras of literature, the time of Voltaire, Rousseau, or even later. You have Bernard Shaw, Strindberg, or Anatole France. What was the glory of these men? It was criticism, and at the same time it was the highest class of art, and at the same time it was fight. You could not think about Bernard Shaw without at the same time thinking of him as a fighting man. In their deepest meaning I think that fighting and the highest class of art conform, and in their deepest meaning they belong together. It may be that there never existed a high class of art without this mysterious combination.

I think that architectural communion, discussion, and contact, and what we say to the public should be the same as with those literary men. Of course, literature and architecture are very, very far from each other, sometimes out of each other's sight.

What are the main obstacles that are stopping us from getting 100 percent production? I cannot deal with them all, but I will pick a few things that might be of the sort that could be eliminated.

First of all, there is the enormous difficulty of educating people to architecture. It requires a command of many fields, an unusually high cultural standard, before you can get a response and get people to understand. I was once very proud when I saw in England a little book for schools giving preliminary education in architecture. It was for very young children in an elementary school. I think it is good to do that, but I am afraid that architecture that covers all the formal and structural world that is around us is too complicated to be an educational thing on the children's level. Probably giving some lectures in architecture to seven- or eight-year-old children is the same thing as teaching sex in the first grade of a primary school.

I think that we could give quite good education on the upper level, but I think it should not go the same way as ordinary art criticism. We may lose our horizontal line if it goes that way. The art critic is today about 100 years old. The habit of writing critical articles about single artists may not be much older. It is growing in the press and it will continue in the same way. It will just be criticism of individual cases, and the real line will be lost. The real line is to plan and to build for the little man, for his benefit.

We may find that the best methods are real examples. Let's say we should do a little group of housing and so on, as experiments, and let people see them. We are working in a very unlucky field in the sense that we do not first have laboratory time before building. We are the only ones in the modern industrial world who have to have the design and directly build it. There should be a laboratory period between those two things. It can be done individually but every civilized country should always have a program of experimental cities and experimental buildings as a real nation. England has had things like that from very early on. We could talk of Raymond Unwin, or the Weissenhof in Germany where there was culminating art, individual art, but it was not really meant as a laboratory period between. I do not think we can really educate people on how they should live without having that sort of thing.

Let us take as the second thing the mechanization, the standardization, in our time. You all know of the mechanization of all our lives; it is part of democracy. It is the only way to give more people more things. But we know that at the same time mechanization and standardization often bring down quality. This means that biologically democracy is a very difficult process. We cannot give to everybody the same quality as we can give to a few people, as was done in the past.

Once Madame Aalto, on a trip abroad, had a discussion with a great industrialist. He said that he had a wonderful new idea of real rationalization in a field where no standardization, no rationalization existed before. He said,

"Have you seen how many steamships and boats are transporting coffee from Brazil to other countries? It is an unpractical way. Coffee is a natural product and is not a rationalized product." He had thirty patents covering a method of pressing a cubic meter of coffee into one little pill that would reduce the tonnage of ships required for its transport to 5 percent of those used. It really was wonderful rationalization. It was a really great result of human thinking. But Madame Aalto asked, "What about the coffee—how does it taste?" And the reply was, "Oh, that is the one bad thing, it doesn't taste right."

That, in a nutshell, shows the enormous difficulties that we have, in keeping every man in the street on the same level and giving him equality. It is even more difficult when we go from material qualities to qualities of the spirit. There the world looks very bad today.

But there are possibilities of using standardization and rationalization for the benefit of the human being. The question is, what should we rationalize and what should we standardize? We could make standards that raise not only the living standard but the spirit too. One very important thing would be if we could create an elastic standardization, a standardization that did not command us, but one that we would command. Slowly, slowly there is more and more mechanical dictatorship over us. We cling to philosophical methods, and in this case, if we would command the material, the philosophy's name would be architecture and nothing else, and we could create a standardization that would have human qualities. We could try things that give more to human beings. It does not matter how much electric cables or the wheels of motorcars are standardized, but when we come to the home, to the things that are close to us, the problem is different—it becomes a question of the spirit, it becomes a question of what intellectual standardization involves.

Once I tried to standardize staircases. Probably that is one of the oldest of standardizations. Of course, we design new staircase steps every day in connection with all our houses, but a standardized step depends on the height of the buildings and on all kinds of things. You cannot use the same step over all, because it has to be elastic enough to be put in everywhere. We tried to solve the matter by an elastic system in which the steps were going into each other, but in such a way that the proportion of the horizontal plane to the vertical plane always kept the formula that we have had since the time of the Renaissance, I think, from Giotto, and even earlier from the Periclean time. For the movement of a human being there is a special rhythmical form. You can't make a step any way you like; it must be a special proportion. I spoke about that in the University at Gothenburg. The Rector said, "Stop for a while, I want to go to the library." He went downstairs to the library and came out with a book—Dante's *Divine Comedy*. He opened it at the page where it says that the worst thing in the Inferno is that the stairs had the wrong proportions.

It is from those little things that we should build a harmonious world for people. There are possibilities if everybody would try to do that and would try to get the officials just to follow our line.

I will make one more point: it is that we are always working with very large sums of money. Everything we do means a large investment. City planning probably is the biggest. Simply to change traffic is today such an expensive thing that people cannot politically get to the point of changing it. We know today that the little man on the street has automobiles all around him. Every minute, even in the smaller towns, hundreds of motor machines are passing the pedestrian, the little man. He is in a much worse position than the engineers who spend eight hours a day in a paper factory. In a paper factory generally there are no motors, only electricity, and if there are motors, there are very few. But on the street there are hundreds passing one all the time. Our streets and cities were designed for completely different purposes—as was the nice Boulevard Italien, for horse traffic, a few horses here and there. Now it's full of automobiles—and we know that they are not neutral. They are putting out a very dangerous heavy gas that lies on the streets. Almost all of my friends in the medical profession think that today we are paying a very

high price for our inability to build a new traffic system in which pedestrians and automobiles are far away from one another, not to speak of housing and living—which should be very far from that. The answer is cancer. The price that we pay for our streets is in the bills for the enormous hospitals that are being built all over the world today.

Then there is our old enemy, the speculator in real estate. That is enemy number one of the architect. But there are other enemies too who may be even more difficult to defeat. For instance, we have in my country—and there are other forms in other countries, for in this matter we are all on the same level—the theoretical line of building economy, which is popularly stated in this way: 'What form of house is most economical?' If we have, let us say, a five-floor, a six-floor, an eight-floor block of flats, there is the question, "How deep should it be? How long? What is the cheapest way we could give people badly needed houses?" Of course, this may be called science. But it is not. The answer is very, very simple—the deepest house is the cheapest. That is clear. One can go further and say that the most inhuman house is the cheapest, that the most expensive light that we have is daylight—let us eliminate that, and then we will get cheaper housing. The most expensive thing is fresh air, because it is not only a question of ventilation, but also a question of city planning. Fresh air for human beings costs acres of ground and good gardens and forests and traffic and meadows.

Real building economy cannot be achieved in this ridiculous way. The real building economy is how much of the good things, at how cheap a cost, we can give. But we should never forget that we are building for human beings. It is the same in all economy—the relationship between the quality of the product and the price of the product. But if you leave out the quality of the product, the whole economy is nonsensical in every field, and it is the same in architecture too.

That sort of line is very suitable for propaganda; propaganda in which the word "economical" is used wrongly, is antihuman. Sometimes it goes so far that it is completely *vice versa*. I know of schools that are turning out stuff on

147

this sort of propaganda line that is probably cheap in figures but very expensive per child.

Let me take another such topic. I jump from the economic consideration to the question of decoration. We all know that there is an independent decorative life in the world. There is industrial art, which has no relationship to the mother, to architecture. It is decoration that you can put everywhere.

It is a very comical thing that wrong rationalization, rationalization made antihuman, the wrong use of the word "economics," and decoration, are the *trois cochons*—they work together. A week ago in Switzerland I saw large lines of buildings made to a mechanical standard without any spirit, but a good marriage with decoration was there to cover things that otherwise would look too hard and too inhuman.

But this triangle of activity leads to an uncultured society and noncultural buildings—this combination of three things that do not belong together. We get an unorganic society. We should work for simple, good, undecorated things, but things that are in harmony with the human being and organically fitted to the little man in the street.

Transcript of a speech given to the Royal Institute of British Architects, 1957

148

73. Church in Wolfsburg, study, 1959

150

75. Auditorium, Technical University, Helsinki, 1960

76. Church and town hall, Seinäjoki, c. 1961

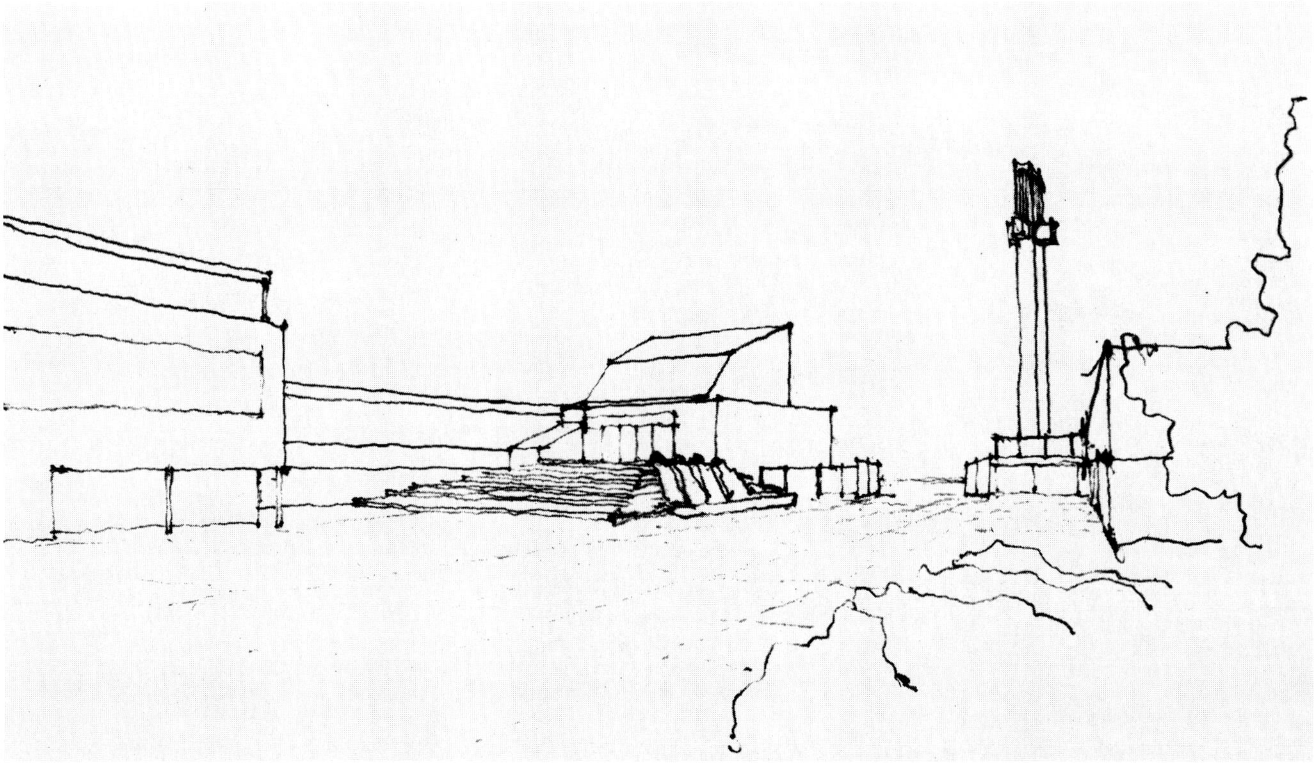

154

FORUM REDIVIVUM / B

79. Perspective, Pensions Institute, competition drawing, 1948

80. Perspective, Pensions Institute, competition drawing, 1948

FORUM REDIVIVUM

The Architect's Conception of Paradise

Ladies and gentlemen. It is difficult to give a speech and still more difficult if it is a jubilee speech because one should absolutely have a theme, but themes don't grow on every tree. In addition I have to limit my speech. One of our friends—I think that many of us at least in theory are his friends—the French painter Georges Braque said once that the most interesting and captivating thing about painting is that one never knows what will become of the painting when one begins painting it. The same is true of my speech, or if you allow, my informal talk. I have not the slightest idea of how it will end. It is appropriate here by the Danish channel. If it were foggy and we drifted ashore we wouldn't know whether the current would take us to Danzig or Malmö or to some other city. But we need something tangible to hold onto, preferably a central idea, even with the risk that we don't know where it will end.

If I am not mistaken this part of the country was a player in a historic tragedy in the manner of the partitions of Poland. This originally Danish region, Skåne, was at one time held in very high regard. I believe it was one of the north's truly great men, Linné, who once fantasized that paradise lay approximately where Malmö now lies. I have not had time to check this information but I have a fairly clear recollection that Linné, proceeding from his botanical premises, philosophized that Skåne combined in an excellent manner all the high-class advantages that one otherwise doesn't find at closer quarters than on especially beautiful Mediterranean shores. In other words, we are theoretically standing on the foundation of paradise. One cannot, I suppose, question the authority of Linné. And perhaps this will give us reason to talk a bit about architecture, or, more simply, the art of building.

Architecture has an ulterior motive, which always lurks, so to speak, around the corner: the thought of creating a paradise. It is the only purpose of our houses. If we did not always carry this thought around with us all our houses would become simpler and more trivial and life would become . . . would it be at all worth living? Each house, each product of architecture that is worthwhile as a symbol is an endeavor to show that we want to build an earthly paradise for people.

So much for the conception of paradise, which perhaps isn't altogether up to date. The man on the street is more interested in how many balls we can shoot into the stratosphere, ordinary basketballs—well, perhaps the main thing is to succeed in getting something up there. And the more we occupy ourselves with these purely theoretical games in the wide blue yonder the more we forget Mother Earth, where man, after all, has his habitat and where happiness—in any case the temporal—is to be created. When one reads the daily papers one gets a funny feeling of Jules Verne in mass circulation. Expensive games are being played. An average rocket costs so much that for the price one could rebuild Malmö, perhaps even twice over. So it is architecture with its paradisiac intention which is decidedly the cheapest game mankind ever played.

In more recent times there have been attacks against architecture. This trend has culminated in Finland, where a few second-class building technicians who don't have the backbone technicians should have, have attacked architecture because it hasn't, in their opinion, sufficiently striven for building economy. But each baroque palace, however overdecorated it may be, is yet a cheaper game than the one that is being played with motors, airplanes, and rockets. Architecture is the cheapest game. It is a game that, if we disregard the major religious epochs, most closely strives to realize a true humanism in our world, to create the very limited happiness one can offer man.

This game is cheap because, among other reasons, architecture has certain advantages over other arts. I began with Georges Braque and don't in any way want to deny the value of painting; on the contrary. But you cannot live in a painting. You cannot make love to a beautiful woman in a painting, not even one who is beautiful and intelligent, or just intelligent. There is not room enough in the picture plane. One can also hardly do it in a sculpture, for that matter. I tried once, but it did not succeed. It was at the top of the Statue of Liberty in America, but I had so many rivals that I found it best to retreat. But in a house, which

perhaps is never such an artistic game, one can in any case live. There is room for many forms of happiness both in the worst-designed palace and the cheapest hut. And here we finally have architecture's synthesis: if we succeed in concentrating its enormous possibilities then we can, by playing with them all, like the world's poets, create physical happiness for people in all its different forms. It is not a bad goal; on the contrary, it is probably the highest under the stratosphere.

What, then, does our conception of paradise look like? In reality we must constantly watch ourselves so that we don't go too far. Exaggerations these days do not show up in the decor, at the level of representation, in formal play or charm, but unfortunately at the technical level, along the lines of shooting basketballs into space. We experiment on a very wide front in order, as one says, to bring the building of dwellings and building technology economically within reach of large masses of people; cheaper apartments, cheaper factories, cheaper houses at different levels. Such an assortment of all imaginable standard products—"prefabrication in all forms"—which we have at the present time, has never before existed. It is impossible to keep a tally of all these results but I fear that the bookkeeping would show a fairly sizable deficit if we could actually work out the index of happiness per individual and workday. Now, in other words, our main task is to find a sensible line; technology in service to man.

I will take an example. In the final analysis it is true that what is called democracy but can't quite be defined—there are philosophers who consider that democracy today is in decline—aims at giving everyone greater freedom. What else could it possibly be, considering the poor craftsmen fifty to one hundred years ago in an area where there were hardly any roads, workers who worked twelve-hour days, etc. A social renewal on an economic foundation—an eight-hour day, more and more social benefits even for the farmer. Philosophically all this means that people have greater freedom. People can use four hours for themselves instead of having to slave away for an employer during those hours.

What is the state of freedom these days, anyway? If in order to make dwellings 4 percent cheaper we have to mechanize building methods so that each element, without the help of the human hand, is lifted from the assembly line directly into place, we arrive, strangely enough, at a borderline where there is a question of how far freedom can be taken before its curve begins to drop. Far-reaching mechanization leads directly to dictatorship. If we only build rationally it will be necessary to place buildings close together, and then we will not be able to bring about the decentralization that would benefit people. A person cannot live on the shore by the little lake; he cannot choose the site for his house. The building site will become a railroad yard. We may state the matter less harshly, but ideologically this is what will happen.

"Cheaper" is a philosophical trap, very dangerous, because a far-reaching technology automatically leads to an administrative dictatorship, totally independent of a political dictatorship. A well-organized industrial system must be managed hierarchically, and in no other way. This is the punishment for Western man's self-righteousness. We now stand at a crossroads. Everyone should have a clear picture of how dangerous the situation is on our globe. It can happen that countries that are not going through the same development process as we will discover other technical aids that allow freedom for man to choose his life style. It has not yet been tried out systematically (I am thinking of the Chinese peasant), but the way in which all cultures rise and fall shows that it is quite possible that something will arrive on the scene to compete with and destroy that which is all too logical in Western development.

I will take one more example. If we build in Malmö, in Copenhagen, or in Helsinki 60 to 70 percent of the building task will have practically nothing to do with the process of building itself. First and foremost the financing of the building presupposes a complicated system of square meter measurements; the dwelling may not be greater than 57 square meters or 89 square meters, or certain figures may not be less than so and so. The government approves the appropriation, and all the financing follows more or less the same system. How have we arrived at this scale according to which a certain dwelling has to be exactly 57 square meters and one that is built to higher social standards has to be 89 square meters? These figures are not empirical; rather, they are office figures. Someone has arrived at them by working from some average figure, and now they stand in the way of our building designs. During the last two years I have had experiences that have proved that if I hadn't been dependent on these figures, I would have achieved solutions that would have given a considerably higher living standard than was achieved by following these office figures. I have recounted this merely as an example of regulations that have nothing to do with true creative work but to which we are subject.

We are carrying a dead weight that appears socially acceptable but can't guarantee the future, the curve that would always rise. And yet day after day there continues an enormous struggle at all the drafting boards where buildings are designed. Sometimes the victories won at these drafting tables succeed in overcoming some of the harmful anomalies. We cannot say that the anomalies are caused by a badly functioning administration. They have come about by themselves. We have come to a theoretical dead end. But victories are won, houses are built where people can lead happy lives; there should just be more such victories. They are won only by concentrating on human happiness. In each detail a chance for joy is welcome. But we have to discard as much as possible of the dead weight that keeps us from creating a humane architecture.

As I said, it is the world's cheapest and surely the world's most beautiful game.

Lecture given at a Swedish city planners' meeting in Malmö, 1957

159

Instead of an Article

The editors of *Arkkitehti* have insisted on a few lines by the undersigned for this issue. However, as I cannot write an article, this dialogue is intended to replace it. It is only partially authentic, but that, of course, is also the case with the classical dialogues.

Sigfried Giedion: "What do I see, old friend, are you planning to write?"

Alvar Aalto: "Planning and planning. I have no choice; I am compelled to."

G. "How awful. I thought you were just about the only architect who doesn't write, but only builds. Are you really serious?"

A. "It's not that serious, but write I must. Because the editors insist, my sense of tact tells me I can't withdraw."

G. "But what are you thinking of writing?"

A. "I don't know."

G. "You've been a teacher, one would think that you'd be able to throw something together."

A. "For me, to say 'I don't know' is a serious matter. Just in the capacity of teacher, in America, I should have lectured and written. My students wanted to learn, preferably everything. They asked, among other things, how one creates good art. I replied, 'I don't know.' The consequences were shattering. One fine day the parents of one of my former students appeared for a meeting with the professor. The first thing they said was: 'We're shelling out $700.00 per term for our talented son's education and his professor says "I don't know."' It was, judging by everything, the end of my short teaching career."

G. "But you have also written poems. Hand one of them in, and you'll get off lightly."

A. "Dear friend, you don't know what you are talking about. The Creator created paper for drawing architecture on. Everything else is, at least for my part, to misuse paper. *Torheit*, as Zarathustra would have said. Of course I have written poems. A few, but, naturally, good ones. But they are written in sand. And poems written in the sand are not suitable for publishers and journals. Their publisher is the wind, a splendid publisher."

(Socrates: So it is with all art forms. Each one avails itself of speech. But only speech that truly concerns itself with something that belongs to the given artistic task. There are also artistic endeavors where speech is out of place, they are created in total silence.)

A. "In other words, I will not publish any poems. I would prefer to see my working drawings published, but they are too detailed and do not fit in this context."

G. "But shouldn't you get something said?"

A. "Architecture's horoscope today is such that my words become negative and that isn't very pleasant. Parallelopipeds of glass and synthetic materials, the inhuman dandy-purism of the big cities, has led irrevocably to a fashionable architecture, which is a dead end."

G. "But despite this there still exists a living, humane architecture."

A. "It exists, yes, but the architecture I just mentioned is highly popular in a naive world. And worse, it has caused a reaction in the opposite direction, an uncritical, clumsy search for novel forms. Housing estates with artificially varied building masses, a motley flora of motifs that don't correspond to the valuable and biologically beautiful variability intrinsic in humans. Often they appear to be more like commercial fairs, and as for public buildings, a propagandistic formalism is pushing itself into the foreground, an architectural equivalent of the terrible lack of balance of the American luxury car and of industrial design in general. Grownup children playing with curves and tensions that they are unable to control. It smells of Hollywood."

Man is forgotten . . . and yet true architecture exists only where man stands in the center. His tragedy and his comedy, both.

In order to lighten the foregoing, a small, gentle postscript: A great scientist, of an international reputation, is taking an afternoon nap in an easy chair in his exclusive club. A mischievous ray of sunshine awakens him. Opposite happens to sit a man whom he doesn't know. The great man gets up and, as if still in a dream, shouts in a thunderous voice, "Sir, can you save me from Vällingby?"

Arkkitehti-Arkitekten, 1958

Speech for the Hundred-Year Jubilee of the Jyväskyla Lycée

Jyväskyla Lycée was founded during the second half of the nineteenth century, which all over the world appears as a remarkable epoch because of the fact that so much of our own era has its origins there. Among others, it brought forth in embryonic form almost all the problems from which our own problems stem. It was during this time that information mediation (education) got started on a large scale. In Finland it was the so-called popular enlightenment that made its active beginnings. Through information mediation became possible the breakthrough of technology and industrialism, the development of which has since without break remolded our living habits and our society's social structure.

An outside observer would obviously notice first the contribution Jyväskyla Lycée made during its first active decades, to spread knowledge to new and wider circles. The emphasis lay apparently on a civilizing level.

Such a goal was criticized even then in a way that was sometimes justified but just as often involved a reactionary effort to stop civilization's march forward. The most important point this critique had to make was that a culture that aims only at mediating and spreading knowledge is too one-sided. It must be complemented with a general presentation (definition) of the democratic classless society, whose features still cannot be fully defined. But for such a classless society to arise, it is necessary, at least during its beginning stages, to accept a technologically oriented and mechanized life style that is a prerequisite for the real achievement of equality. The mechanized life style is in other words a peripheral phenomenon of civilization, a phenomenon that a growing civilization cannot control. Civilization threatens, in other words, to become uncivilized. In order for this whole complex of problems—civilization, the classless society, technomechanical aids—to be solved in a positive way from a human viewpoint, a stronger element is needed, something more inviting than civilization as such. A mystical element is needed, something that has been called culture and that has its roots both in the instincts and in something learned that cannot, however, be mediated through the educational process, as it is spontaneously born through a process of accumulation that no one has yet succeeded in explaining. It has been said that only this concept of culture takes account of the factors that can influence society in the right direction and make a mark on its new way of functioning. Only in this way can the internal contradictions be overcome and the little man given humane living conditions.

It is clear to an outside observer that Jyväskyla Lycée, our own hundred-year-old school, was a civilizing factor, even in the matter of its methods. The question is simply whether it was in too one-sided a way. To my perception it wasn't, and I hope that it isn't today.

If we examine Jyväskyla Lycée's spiritual profile to the extent that such a thing can be graphically presented, we can conclude that there are certain features which indicate that the spread of civilization was complemented all along by that mystical, cumulative force through which culture arises.

To begin with, the program of instruction contained so many different elements that the school can in no way be regarded as a purely utilitarian educational institution, whose goal is to be an exclusive mediator of practical formulas for different tasks or problems.

In my time, the language instruction covered—and presumably still covers—a wide range, all the way from the classical languages to today's world languages. This alone was an indirect factor for advancing culture, in that the students were unavoidably presented with a many-sided viewpoint for judging life's many phenomena. The result was something akin to what Goethe meant by the expression *ausser sich gehen*. Such a phenomenon cannot—or at least not as easily—arise in countries where higher education is based on only one language.

Ausser sich gehen, the experience of seeing and judging from other points of view than one's own person and one's own milieu, encourages doubt and skepticism. The much-discussed skeptical world view is in reality a necessary condition for anyone who would like to make a cultural contribution. This is of course dependent on skepticism's transformation into a positive phenomenon, an unwilling-ness to "move with the stream." On a higher level skepticism is transformed into its apparent opposite, to love with a critical sensibility. It is a love that lasts, as it rests on a critically tested foundation. It can result in such a love for the little man that it functions as a kind of guardian when our era's mechanized life style threatens to strangle the individual and the organically harmonious life.

From this same speaker's platform was once delivered a lecture that I attended as a young lycée student. It was our French teacher who for the first time planted the positive seeds of skepticism in our souls. He talked about stupidity and those who exposed it, starting with Erasmus and ending with Voltaire. An educational institution that educates its students by such many-sided methods not only disseminates civilization but also advances culture.

I said at the beginning of my lecture that civilization is followed by technology and therefore leads to a mechanized life style. In order for the same civilization, the same advantages, that formerly only a few citizens could enjoy to be distributed equally throughout the whole society, an enormous, as it were mechanical, apparatus is needed. Despite the fact that this process has not yet reached its end, the apparatus today is already so big that having "created" the new society it now threatens to strangle its original purpose. If a strong, culturally oriented general will doesn't intercede and steer our lives in a better direction, the beautiful rising curve of civilization will rapidly sink to its own demise.

We cannot determine the exact makeup of the cultural consensus, but we can to a certain extent lay down its conditions and goals. Perhaps it could be stated in the following manner: it is not likely that deep down our era's technomechanical civilization is stamped by an insoluble contradiction. It must be possible to humanize technology. It must be possible to bring it closer to the little man's world. Those too-mechanized phenomena that are foreign to our sensibilities can be given a less aggressive character so that they serve man's life more harmoniously. But this can happen only if we are always prepared, through all life's shifts, to engage in skepticism and critical activity. It is necessary to take the little man's frame of reference and what benefits him as a positive yardstick for everything we do.

A further condition is that the concept of culture not be misunderstood or misused. It is not an isolated phenomenon that can be divorced from life. There should not exist so-called cultural divisions among people and special decorative elements in our environment, as culture is the thread that runs through all things. Even the most modest everyday task is of such a nature that it can be humanized and given cultural harmony.

A few days ago, when one of my churches (the church at Vuoksenniska) was consecrated, Bishop Martti Simojaki said in his remarks, "Christianity should not isolate itself from its followers; it belongs to all, both those who believe and those for whom nothing is sacred."

One could suggest something similar as a program for the humanizing cultural consensus. The deepest culture is in reality that which expresses itself in everyday life and all its forms. As an isolated phenomenon it means nothing.

I believe that our hundred-year-old Jyväskyla Lycée has in this respect made a unique contribution.

When, during the late-medieval flowering, the cathedral raised itself in every city above the insignificant buildings' tight confusion, it was a symbol for life's ungraspable, difficult unity. In later times these cathedrals have been freed from the surrounding confusion of houses, with the unexpected result that the cathedrals' forms have lost their strength.

In its way something similar has happened with my school. It lacks, of course, higher architectural qualities, but it was instead a spiritual phenomenon surrounded by the confusion of everyday life. The school commenced every fall under the sign of the surrounding market life—it lies of course near the former horse market. The contrast that made itself manifest at the time has something in common with the paradoxical unity that united the cathedral with its surrounding confusion of housing. The school served life by being a contrasting phenomenon and ap-

parently succeeded in making its contribution to our era's most difficult task: to protect the little man.

Address given in 1958; not previously published

164

Town Planning and Public Buildings

Colleagues, ladies and gentlemen. This is not a lecture. Architecture is such a comprehensive conception that it is difficult to find the theme for a unified lecture. This is just an introductory remark. Not even those are always easy to formulate. We all know, of course, that when something that has been explained in words is implemented in reality, in matter, it can be muddled in many ways, as happened when a youth organization in a Finnish village made the decision that only beautiful houses should be allowed in the village. The only question left unanswered was what was beautiful. And that question has remained unanswered.

I shall begin with a conversation, even though it took place in another language. I asked a friend and colleague: Have you ever seen a beautiful city, or something more than that; an organic and well-functioning city, in short, a good city? I received no answer. I then proceeded to state that I had never seen a beautiful city. There are some good city districts, districts to be valued, sometimes very insignificant parts of the city in question; but for the city as a whole, as for all human creations, Göran Schildt's observation that man's treatment of nature reminds one of a cancer seems valid; it always involves a certain amount of destruction. Some examples of places that are close to perfect: Piazza San Marco in Venice has in almost all respects succeeded in mirroring the citizenship accurately, even the tourists, of whom there are about ten times as many as inhabitants. And a city like Siena is markedly organic and as such unsurpassed.

Human creations are, in other words, not perfect, and the fact that we believe that there is a plethora of beautiful cities in the world depends only on which details we criticize. If we apply high standards we won't find any perfect city.

I said that there are good city districts. For example, northern Spain's medieval cities, which look like bacteria cultures, function as a perfect shell for people's lives. We have many other good examples. In other words, there is much for us to do if we wish to achieve better results than today's. Our discussion of cities deals first with problems. Exhibitions, lectures, one after another address problems that, naturally, like all problems, are of a passing nature in the sense that they are replaced by others.

I recently returned from Siena, which in my opinion meets some fairly high standards of what a good city should be. The city of Siena is singular to the extent that, although it is built on a hill, like the Tuscan cities in general, the hill is not a round pot but is branched out and formed like a hand. Only necessary service traffic is allowed in the city, and development trends indicate that Siena is the only city that will be able to solve its traffic problems without difficulty. Its three lions—the town hall's graceful tower, the *duomo*'s black and white facade, and the *fortezza*, which is one of the tallest—also give the city facial features that simply make life there more pleasant.

We are presently building more public buildings than before in Finland. We know that independent Finland has built extremely few public buildings. This is true of most of the cities in the country. It was not long ago that the only public building in Helsinki was the Diet building. Even such public institutions as the state bank share space with rental apartments. A common combination was once a government office and a movie theater. This for economic reasons! But these economic calculations do not make sense today. Perhaps they may still appear profitable on the treasurer's balance sheet, but profitability has some negative consequences. It deprives the city of its identity: nose, ears, mouth, and hands. Such features must stand out separately; they should not melt together into one great mass. It disturbs the sense of place in the city and causes a number of other problems. Among these, traffic problems have become most complicated because there isn't enough space reserved for public buildings and because cities have taken the form of concrete slabs based on a rental housing psychology.

This situation has another consequence. In Finland people are, in a way, unused to public buildings; this is true of the architectural profession as well as the society at large. I don't mean that in Finland there aren't a large number of people who have nothing against public build-

ings and who have both the desire and the ability to build them, but in general it is a fact that people are unused to public buildings. The difference between Finland and, for example, the countries of central Europe lies in the fact that planning of public buildings here goes through the same stages as the planning of an apartment house or a warehouse, in other words, each in its turn: regional planning, master planning, town planning, and detailed town planning. And only after all that does one get to the building. The building, in other words, comes last. In Finland the city lacks legal sovereignty. Not until it has been dealt with by all too many authorities can its face take form.

I have, for instance, never heard any drawn-out hearings on a town planning change or on projects for public buildings in Wolfsburg, a city somewhat smaller than Tampere. For the city council a five-minute presentation sufficed. Yes, such a town center we will build. It had been announced publicly and each member of the city council was familiar with the matter. The councilmen came and looked at the piles when they had been driven but no red tape was required during the whole construction period.

The problems, naturally, are complicated. Finland's laws are not too bad, but they are naturally made to prevent misuse. In general it is exactly for that purpose that one passes a law. The law cannot count on quality. One cannot decide that a good building will be let off more easily. The same is true of people and criminal laws. One cannot take into consideration possible good personality traits in a criminal. As I remember, I once talked to Professor Wahlman about this during my time in Viipuri, and he pointed out that a building plan is naturally binding but that the law has been passed to prevent misuse. It would be a good thing if we were able to achieve the possibility for flexibility in this respect. Unfortunately we don't even always know ahead of time whether a building is good or bad. It is impossible. I wish, however, that Finland's Architectural Association would give thought to flexibility, which should be included as a useful element in both the building codes and in our work.

I just said that we were unused to public buildings. Finland's independence has been so filled with diverse problems that this is quite understandable. In working on the housing problem, we have been forced to ignore the public sector. The housing question, however, is not an isolated problem. Housing must be complemented by all those buildings intended for common use.

We are now living in a time of crisis to the extent that we have to correct our attitude toward public buildings. Among the public building's most important tasks is to stand as an example for the secular building, in other words, for houses and housing complexes. Even in this area one can see our unfamiliarity with public buildings. We strive to achieve an originality in them that perhaps isn't wrong in itself—on the contrary, it is an excellent thing—but that very often causes the public building to stand out from the community instead of functioning as a model. It lacks the force of example, the right effect on the secular level. Now clearly I don't mean a direct example, so that the forms would be identical. The connection should be much deeper, and the effect indirect.

I have just spoken of flexibility, and I would like to add something, namely, that a harmonious community can be created only by trying to make it so in as thorough a manner as possible. This way of thinking implies also that public buildings and average buildings for everyday life must stand in a certain implicit harmony with one another and that, when we move to the public building sector, we don't have the right to do precisely what we want. This is a responsibility that applies to the whole society.

But the dwelling, which has been architecture's main concern for as long as my diploma has been in the Polytechnic's archives, should in no case be forgotten. It is just as important as it ever has been. But it, like the public building, suffers to some extent from the many difficulties caused by the many different authorities that have to approve it. If we want to build a housing complex next to a small town, the phases we must go through are as follows: the regional plan, the general plan, and the town plan, in addition to the eventual changes and finally the construction period. The human psyche is so exhausted after all these phases have been negotiated that the very quality of building is put at risk.

The building is the best-defined element in city planning, and thus in the whole area of activity where city plans and building plans belong, and it should therefore not be relegated to last place. It seems perhaps too sarcastic a joke if I say, "Dwellings first and the town plan afterwards." But this is the way the Spanish medieval cities that I have mentioned and many others came about—it is true, not totally without plan, since there was some direction although we cannot analyze exactly how it functioned. Between the building and the clusters of buildings that sprang up there was a certain interaction, but today it is lacking. Building should be initiated from both ends. When we begin regional and general planning we should also begin with the design of buildings. We should know what to include in our plan. The fact that we have existing buildings, prototypes, etc. means that architecture is a field with no possibility of developing itself further because architecture doesn't have an experimental phase. We have practically no place to experiment, or the ones we have are so tied down by a plethora of other tasks that they do not serve an experimental purpose. My own advice—if I may even give advice—would be that the same principle of flexibility that is applied to public buildings—to siting them, creating them, and, from a psychological point of view, incorporating them with housing complexes—also should be applied to further the work of the architectural profession. When we plan a larger building cluster for a certain area, a neutral area that could serve as an experimental field can be separated from this overall area. There we could immediately begin to build—naturally, not a large number of buildings—while working on the totality that still exists only on paper. In this manner we would become familiar with the elements of which a community consists.

I am ending my speech by directing these hopes for flexibility to my colleagues and to the authorities who to such a great extent influence the building up of Finland.

167

"Kaupunkisuunnitelu ja julkiset rakennukset," speech given at the Finnish Architectural Association's Congress for Planning of Greater Helsinki, April 22, 1966

National–International

The theme of this issue of *Arkkitehti*, "National and International," is, for architecture or any of the other arts, difficult to pursue in depth. Superficially the concepts *national* and *international* are regarded as opposites; in a deeper sense this is less plausible.

Each person, however, is born in a particular defined area. His starting point is national; even more limited than that, he is presumably born within four walls. It follows that his starting point isn't a nation but is of lesser scope, a locality. From this local starting point a person's career takes him wider afield—the local context can become national, and the national, international. This development always spreads out from a given point, rather like rings in the water. The extension is, however, not absolute. The starting point and the outer limit stand in some kind of relationship to each other.

In art it is almost unnecessary to discuss such a basic issue. Perhaps the Erechtheum was originally national, but it has become international. So it is with all art. The end is always within a wider sphere than the starting point, but that does not prevent the starting point and the end point from being next to each other.

Architecture is not merely national but clearly has local ties in that it is rooted in the earth. Through its forms it can achieve an international influence. When everything is said and done, no matter what the starting point or the end may be, it is the connection between the two concepts that achieves the balance we need in today's world, where the concepts *national* and *international* can hardly be separated from each other.

"Kansallinen-kansainvälinen," *Arkkitehti*, 1967

Sigfried Giedion in Memoriam

There are art historians and critics with a world of ideas and a philosophy that act as a stimulus to the branches of art they are writing about. Sigfried Giedion was just such an actively creative critic, one of the few in either our or past times. He was especially concerned with architecture, though his range included all the visual arts. He was the founder of the Congrès International d'Architecture Moderne (CIAM) and its main intellectual force. His significance for the architecture of the last decades and especially for its critical "breakthrough" period cannot be overemphasized.

But above all, one remembers his personal attitude toward those architects who worked to liberate architecture and to the group they constituted. This personal relationship was especially complete because it combined true friendship with fearless criticism, the most valuable and at the same time most open form a friendship can take. Only such a firm attitude both to person and object can achieve results of a lasting value and at the same time act as an inspiration over a wide creative field.

His deeds will be evaluated and referred to in a wide variety of contexts in the future, and his literary production speaks for itself.

In Giedion's Dolder speech many critical thoughts and influences were born in the shadow of the plane tree's lofty branches, but also encouraging thoughts directed at his architect friends that gave them both strength and courage in their work during a difficult, but at the same time unusually creative, period. He achieved wide-ranging results.

Arkkitehti, 1968

Conversation

Göran Schildt: You usually do not step forward with theoretical programs or explanations but direct those who ask to your buildings. In fact, through your creations you have given your answer to many of architecture's current problems, from the planning of city centers, the proper use of standardization, and the design of the industrial environment all the way to furniture design and interior detailing. The question is simply whether these solutions should be given a more general application than the individual case, if, in other words, they should be regarded as prototypes and general answers.

Alvar Aalto: Each task is different and the solutions can therefore not be made general. The examples I have given remain specific and are relevant in other cases only as a method. So many things in architecture are still at an analytical level. What is needed is synthesis. Nothing is more dangerous than to separate analysis and synthesis; they belong together inextricably.

G. S. You began your career during an era that created the expression, "The house is a machine for living." The evolution away from individual, creative architecture with an artistic aim has, of course, continued at an accelerated pace. The social, economic, technical, and functional demands are regarded by many as sufficient guidelines for design. Do you think that in the future there will be any role for architects, or will the work of engineers suffice?

A. A. I not only think but would say with certainty that architects will be needed more and more. It is another matter whether engineers could become architects if they had the talent. The task is to find an overall vision that can never emerge from an analysis of an architectural program. One cannot for example study traffic problems by themselves, or comfort factors by themselves. "The buildings first and then the city plan" is a paradox with which I once provoked some colleagues.

G. S. You believe, in other words, that the architect is one of society's guides with the power to steer development on to sound paths and correct the drawbacks of our technical civilization?

A. A. One could say, if one wanted to make phrases, that the architect should seek his task in attempting to humanize technology. But I am on the whole against the tendency to create an opposition between architects and engineers; it is more a question of making the collaboration harmonious. I have even been the mediator in Brazil in a dispute between the two professions where the position of the engineers was not the lesser.

G. S. There are sometimes complaints that architects in Finland show a tendency to ignore social concerns and to devote themselves instead to artistry and irresponsible effect seeking. Do you consider the critique to have some justification?

A. A. To some extent. But the social sphere is not something that can be guarded as a separate sector; it must be built inextricably into the artistic.

G. S. In other words, you feel that it is not through intensified sociological or psychological research, but through the intuition of visionaries, that our era's architectural problems can be solved?

A. A. The latter is a more direct route. Analysis can be sidetracked, not just on one but on many false paths.

G. S. In your youth did you consider yourself a revolutionary banner carrier for new ideas in opposition to an established tradition? Do you now feel yourself to be a defender of traditional values against eagerly protesting youth? I pose the question because your architecture totally lacks polemical features—it is as if you worked totally undisturbed or totally uninterested in others' work or opinions.

A. A. European culture has to a remarkable degree been based on a kind of professional protest. We can think of Luther, Newton, Galileo, or the French authors of the Enlightenment. They also show that one cannot remain at the level of protest; a synthesis, an alternative must be provided. Dilettantish protests against what has gone before are like striking at thin air, like the question "Are you modern or old fashioned?"—superficial. One should protest with one's projects, not with phrases.

G. S. It is of course difficult to chart the influences from

older colleagues that are the point of departure for each artistic effort, but it would be interesting despite this to hear your viewpoint on the role that, for example, Eliel Saarinen, Gunnar Asplund, Frank Lloyd Wright, and Le Corbusier played in yours.

A. A. Very difficult to say. Most of them I didn't know of at all when I began my career and chose my direction. But naturally there is an interplay among colleagues. As far as Saarinen is concerned, there was no mutual understanding. Among the older Finnish architects I am perhaps most grateful to Sigurd Frosterus and Gustave Strengell. They were not the ones who discovered me—that I did myself—but they were the first who understood me and gave me recognition. Also I have a high degree of respect for Gunnar Asplund. I met him on my first trip to Sweden in 1923. We became friends and I saw his Skandia theater. As far as Wright is concerned I knew nothing about him until I came to the U.S.A. in 1939 and saw his buildings for the first time. The Bauhaus has never interested me; more so Jugend in its continental origins, Henry van de Velde and the others. Le Corbusier reached me indirectly as a general feeling in the air during these years. He had for the most part expressed himself in books and with books it is as I once said in a conversation with General Talvela. He told me he doesn't read books about war, but rather about art and architecture. I confessed that I gladly read books about war but never about architecture.

G. S. In the outside world you are known as *the* Finnish architect, but here at home you have been the most internationally active and oriented. Do you regard yourself as bringing to the fore some special Finnish tradition and as representing a locally rooted architectural conception?

A. A. I don't think I have a feeling for folklore. The traditions that bind us lie more in the climate, in the material conditions, in the nature of the tragedies and comedies that have touched us. I do not make an ostentatious Finnish architecture and do not in any way see an opposition between Finnish and international. My country belongs to Europe, if that isn't saying too much.

G. S. Building design is, of course, seldom a one-man

job but is based in a work group, often on the collective work of a whole, well-organized architecture office. In the case of your office a large number of our best-known architects have begun their career under your leadership. How do you regard the question of collaboration? Have impulses from your coworkers had a decisive effect on your buildings? Is the result in some way to be regarded as a teamwork?

A. A. Teamwork is to me an ominous word. I have seen bad examples of it in many countries. The work that obviously has to be done by a series of coworkers takes place in my office in familiar contexts where everyone understands one another. In certain cases the collaboration reminds one of an orchestra where each instrument should play correctly under the leadership of the conductor and at the same time have its own responsibility and a duty to adhere to a harmony. I owe my many collaborators through the years a large measure of gratitude for having understood this so well.

172 G. S. At the large exhibitions of your work in Florence and in Helsinki the public has had a chance to become acquainted with a significant number of both sculptures and paintings of yours. Do you regard these branches of your activity as independent in relationship to architecture? Do you consider that through them you are able to express something different from what you achieve in your buildings?

A. A. The paintings and the sculptures are a part of my method of working, which is why I unwillingly see them as separated from my architecture, as if they could express something beyond it. Many architects have devoted themselves to painting as a separate activity. For me the situation is different. One could say that I don't regard my sculptures and paintings as something that belongs to these professions. It is difficult to prove from case to case but they are for me branches of the same tree whose trunk is architecture.

G. S. Those who have worked with exhibitions of your work or with studies concerned with your development have often had the impression that you are uninterested in your own past. Why are you so reluctant concerning exhibitions and the writing of history?

A. A. I am not usually so Nietzschean, but in this context the German philosopher deserves to be quoted: "Only obscurantists look back." The work is finished for my part when the building is ready. Yet I would like to say that I make use of the historian's craft, where writings about my earlier projects have been a direct benefit for my work today.

Preface to the Aalto exhibition catalog, Helsinki, 1967